THE WAR BY THE SHORE

THE WAR BY THE SHORE

THE INCOMPARABLE DRAMA OF THE 1991 RYDER CUP

CURT SAMPSON

GOTHAM BOOKS

GOTHAM BOOKS
Published by Penguin Group (USA) Inc.
375 Hudson Street, New York, New York 10014, U.S.A.
Penguin Group (Canada), 90 Eglinton Avenue East, Suite 700, Toronto, Ontario M4P 2Y3, Canada (a division of Pearson Penguin Canada Inc.); Penguin Books Ltd, 80 Strand, London WC2R 0RL, England; Penguin Ireland, 25 St Stephen's Green, Dublin 2, Ireland (a division of Penguin Books Ltd); Penguin Group (Australia), 250 Camberwell Road, Camberwell, Victoria 3124, Australia (a division of Pearson Australia Group Pty Ltd); Penguin Books India Pvt Ltd, 11 Community Centre, Panchsheel Park, New Delhi–110 017, India; Penguin Group (NZ), 67 Apollo Drive, Rosedale, Auckland 0632, New Zealand (a division of Pearson New Zealand Ltd); Penguin Books (South Africa) (Pty) Ltd, 24 Sturdee Avenue, Rosebank, Johannesburg 2196, South Africa

Penguin Books Ltd, Registered Offices: 80 Strand, London WC2R 0RL, England

Published by Gotham Books, a member of Penguin Group (USA) Inc.

First printing, September 2012
10 9 8 7 6 5 4 3 2 1

Unless otherwise noted, all photos are courtesy of Curt Norman.

LIBRARY OF CONGRESS CATALOGING-IN-PUBLICATION DATA
Sampson, Curt.
The war by the shore : the incomparable drama of the 1991 Ryder Cup / Curt Sampson.
p. cm.
ISBN 978-1-592-40796-5 (hardback)
1. Ryder Cup—History. 2. Golf—Tournaments—United States—History. 3. Golf—Tournaments—Europe—History. I. Title.
GV970.3.R93S36 2012
796.352—dc23
2012014288

Printed in the United States of America
Set in Walbaum
Designed by Chris Welch

TO PAT MORROW

CONTENTS

TEAM USA

Dave Stockton
(Captain)

Raymond Floyd

Payne Stewart

Mark Calcavecchia

Paul Azinger

Corey Pavin

Wayne Levi

Chip Beck

Mark O'Meara

Fred Couples

Lanny Wadkins

Hale Irwin

Steve Pate

TEAM EUROPE

Bernard Gallacher
(Captain)

David Feherty

Colin Montgomerie

José María Olazábal

Steven Richardson

Severiano Ballesteros

Ian Woosnam

Paul Broadhurst

Sam Torrance

Mark James

Bernhard Langer

David Gilford

Nick Faldo

INTRODUCTION

We may sometimes try to forget history,
but it does not forget us.

—*Alan Schom in* Napoleon Bonaparte

The 1991 Ryder Cup began in 1985.

Up to then the venerable biennial match between all-star teams of golf professionals was more ceremonial exhibition than real competition, barely more than a periodic ritual to confirm that the axis of golf power had permanently shifted from Europe to the United States. When the first wave of tough young American pros, steeled in the caddie yards, started winning in the late twenties, the game was changed forever. The chivalrous but overwhelmed Brits bore their humiliation with grace but the inevitable outcome had all the drama of afternoon tea. The event's one-sided predictability—the U.S. record from 1935 forward was nineteen wins, one loss, and a tie—kept Cup results buried in the agate amid the bowling scores. The Ryder Cup was never televised live in the States. Reinforcements for the Great Britain/Ireland team had arrived in 1979, when all European pros became eligible, but with no effect on the outcome. The '79 and '81 Cups were the usual snooze.

In 1983, a flicker: NBC deemed the proceedings sufficiently

interesting to televise the final two hours. And they got a hell of a show, because the heretofore overmatched Europeans did so well in the team matches that the thing was tied going into the final day, and then Team Europe forsook its usual Sunday swoon for some vigorous competition in the singles. With the cameras on him and the Cup on the line, up stepped Lanny Wadkins. Oozing attitude and taking little extra time, the plucky Yank slashed at a wedge shot from seventy-three yards on the eighteenth at PGA National. Damn near holed it. Captain Jack Nicklaus smooched his divot, a strange sight. After Tom Watson edged Bernard Gallacher 2 and 1 a minute later, the match was won, but barely. Lanny's teammates and Captain Jack hugged and nearly kissed him as they skipped up the fairway. Lightning streaked the south Florida sky and distant thunder rumbled, a portent.

"Everything changed in 1985," says Mark McCumber. "I recall missing the team when Hubert Green won the PGA, which qualified him automatically and bumped me off. Didn't think anything of it—I was disappointed for about ten minutes." Making the Ryder Cup squad was an honor, to be sure, but it wasn't like getting a knighthood or an Academy Award; in 1977, Tom Weiskopf caused rumbles, but not a Congressional investigation, when he declined his spot in favor of growing a beard and going on a hunting trip in the Yukon. McCumber rose early for three days in mid-September to catch his almost-teammates putting their arms around the Cup once again. What he saw amazed him: At an English countryside course called the Belfry, Team Europe throttled the American side. "We couldn't handle the crowds," explained Captain Lee Trevino, a loser's excuse never heard before. The *crowds*? Trevino also debuted the use of the word *war* to describe the competition.

After the final toasts at the post-Match dinner, Team Europe threw itself fully clothed and fully drunk into the hotel pool. One of the swimmers—a Scottish lad named Sam Torrance—admitted that he stayed pretty well toasted for the next three and a half days.

Two years later in 1987, with much more interest this time, McCumber sat in his living room with a remote control clicker to observe his colleagues help the world make sense again. In the homiest of home games—at Nicklaus's course in Ohio, Muirfield Village, with Jack returning as captain—Europe won again, and for the first time on American dirt. Incredulity all around.

Captain Jack spoke graciously in the aftermath about the fine play of Seve and Nick and Bernhard and Ian. But privately—in his own living room, in fact—he addressed his team in very blunt terms. On that final day, not a single American won or even tied the final hole. Looking directly at Payne Stewart, Captain Jack stated that the cream of American golf had forgotten how to win or had never really learned. "You guys need to grow a pair," he said.

Raymond Floyd, he of the scary competitor's eyes and the strange prancing walk, would captain the 1989 expedition back to the Belfry. By now the desire among players, aficionados, and the American sports media to win back the Cup had become a fever; no one could act blasé about *almost* making the team, and turning down a spot à la Weiskopf was unthinkable. After winning the Players Championship in '88 and the Western Open the following summer, McCumber qualified for the '89 team. A hard grinder who hit the ball like a kicking mule, the Jacksonville native got to see for himself what Trevino and Nicklaus had been talking about: "It was unlike anything I'd ever seen. A football atmosphere. The crowds were incredibly pro-Europe, but still . . . reasonable. I mean, they could appreciate a good shot by an American."

In the afternoon of the second day, McCumber hit a heroic three-wood tee ball to within eight feet of the hole on the par-four tenth, and made the putt for eagle. The gallery applauded as if the American were someone else's kid at a piano recital, which is to say, unenthusiastically, but at least they didn't jeer or call his partner Four Eyes (in that match, McCumber and Tom Kite beat Bernhard Langer and José María Cañizares 2 and 1). But on the same hole in another match, Kite drove his ball to the fringe of the green. A spectator stepped out of the crowd and emphatically stomped on it.

And when Lanny Wadkins was introduced on the first tee, he was booed. "I looked over at my mother," Lanny recalls. "She'd turned white as that napkin."

Before he hit, and while he was being so audibly disapproved of, Wadkins looked over at teammate Peter Jacobsen and mouthed the words "I love it."

Partisanship—for Arnold Palmer or Walter Hagen or whomever—had always been a happy part of watching a golf tournament. But interfering with the play, or cheering someone's mistake, or *booing*? That had always been beyond the pale in golf. It was simply Not Done.

Now, it was Done—starting in '85 at the Belfry and resuming there in '89. (The home fans in Ohio in '87 were so equitable that Nicklaus had to ask them to quit being so darned polite, and he had little American flags distributed to inspire a bit more enthusiasm for Team USA.) Meanwhile, an American screwing up a shot or a putt Over There had his misery compounded by loud bursts of joy and occasionally a snippet of the songs they sing at football matches at Wembley.

As for the pressure: McCumber found that it was, as advertised, suffocating. Since the first Ryder Cup in 1927, participants had been amazed at how playing for one's country and for teammates dehydrated the mouth. Even in the boring old days of certain U.S. victory, hands attempting to tee a ball on the first hole shook as if palsied. Now the athletic stage fright had been ratcheted up beyond recognition. "I'd never felt anything like it," McCumber says. "Not even being in the lead in a major compared."

The crowd involvement and the intensity of emotion made a dangerous combination for two men already wired so tightly that you could pluck them like a mandolin string. Paul Azinger and Seve Ballesteros bickered shockingly throughout their singles match in '89. During the match, Zinger paid Seve the extreme insult of standing near him for every shot he hit from the rough—the clear message being that without monitoring, Seve might foot-massage his ball into a better lie. Seve replied with—or perhaps he opened the bidding with—what came to be known as his "educated cough," a tickle in his throat that flared up at the top of Azinger's backswing. The American won this round, one-up; the two teams tied, and sportsmanship lost. The battle lines had been drawn.

Tickets for the 1991 Ryder Cup at the Ocean Course at Kiawah Island, South Carolina, sold out in less than a week. NBC and USA Network planned to televise every shot, twenty-one and a half hours of live coverage, an exponential increase from any previous Cup. (They would end up showing twenty-four hours.)

McCumber tore cartilage in his knee playing touch football the day he returned from England in September of '89, and the injury was one reason he didn't make the '91 team. NBC asked him to be an on-course reporter—he'd successfully done a bit of TV commentary before—and he accepted. With a brace on his knee and a heavy backpack of audio gear, McCumber exhausted himself clambering over the sand dunes, but he had a great seat for the melodrama and a unique point of view. "It was a little more personal in '91, a little more teetering on the edge," he recalls. "Some of the comments from the gallery were just over the top. And every day in every match was total pressure.

"The Ryder Cup reached as high an emotional pinnacle as it ever could. After that, we knew how good the Europeans were. But back then, we just didn't know."

They found out. Under a South Carolina sun so bright it hurt to look up, the eyes of the world constricted the swings and clouded the judgment of twenty-four international golfers. The vice president of the United States followed the action in person. His boss, Bush the Elder, recorded his "thousand points of light" speech early Saturday morning, then hustled from Washington, D.C., to a resort eighty miles down the coast from Kiawah, the better to feel the emotion as he watched the afternoon fourball. On the morning of the final two days, the president opened the NBC coverage, with a paean to fair play and a reminder that "the Ryder Cup belongs in the USA." On a set in Spain, Sean Connery eschewed any film work in favor of watching every minute of the Cup on a satellite TV. "Compulsive viewing," he recalled. "I have never seen more nail-biting drama"—even, presumably, in his own movies. Gamesmanship, subtle and blunt, included a twenty-minute video of Ryder Cup highlights at the prematch banquet that showed only *U.S.* Ryder Cup highlights. During the competition and afterward, the losing team muttered that they were being cheated; the memoirists among them would document specific charges.

"It was unlike anything I've seen before or since, and I've been going to the Ryder Cup since 1953," says Ben Wright, the longtime golf commentator for CBS TV. "It was the one time it got really ugly, too vicious for words. Corey Pavin in fatigues—such bullshit. If it had gone on that way, the Ryder Cup would have fallen into disrepute."

But what a show! Character and characters were revealed. Emotions redlined. Choking and grace arm-wrestled. The setting amplified everything. Surf sounds and seabirds floated in the air above an ingenious tumble of a golf course. Witnesses to hurricanes, the lonely trees dotted here and there on the Ocean Course were topped by fright wigs of leaves. Some will aver that the 1960 U.S. Open was the best golf tournament ever, and others will put down their drinks to detail the fascinating turns in the plot at the '77 British, the '86 Masters, or the '54 PGA.

But no one votes for the Ryder Cup, even though we watch it

so intently that we almost forget to breathe. Even though we have twelve avatars in the game, not just the one guy whose game or style we like. Even though the cliff-hanger nature of team international match play was once sharpened by personalities and circumstance to an excruciating point.

More than two decades have passed since that unusual weekend in South Carolina. Since then the twenty-four players in the drama have suffered through twelve divorces, a heart attack, two diagnoses of Attention Deficit Disorder, one of alcoholism, one of depression, two of cancer, and a plane crash. Rheumatoid arthritis nearly crippled one; six spinal surgeries immobilized another. Some lost their hair; a couple of others aren't fooling anyone with comb-overs and dye. They lost distance and gained weight. Their children grew up. The divorcés remarried, one of them twice. Two of the group died.

But for three days of furious concentration and focus in September of '91, the past was mere prologue and the future didn't exist. All that mattered was that little gold Cup.

PART ONE
DEPRESSION ELEVEN

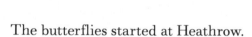

The butterflies started at Heathrow.

—Colin Montgomerie

Two hundred million, twenty-three, and four thousand dollars

—The estimated television viewership of the '91 Ryder Cup, a record; the number of countries getting the live TV feed; the pay for each U.S. team member

1

MONDAY, SEPTEMBER 23, 1991

The afterburners screamed, accelerating the jet to 200 miles per hour, then 220, and still it didn't leave the ground. British Airways Flight 4 would need a couple of miles of Heathrow tarmac and two tons of fuel to achieve liftoff. Boiling air spewed from two giant exhaust manifolds, the light brown billows contrasting with the bright white fuselage. The paint had to be reflective to deal with the heat from the speed and the unfiltered sun at sixty thousand feet.

The English called the fastest, highest-flying, and most beautiful commercial jet ever built Concorde, leaving off the article—just as they go "to hospital" while Americans go to *the* hospital. Cruising at twice the speed of sound, Concorde cut the time of a flight from London to JFK by more than half—from seven hours to about three. A fighter jet of a passenger plane, the needle-nosed, delta-winged Concorde seated only one hundred passengers in twenty-five rows of two by two. Its windows and storage bins were tiny, its leather seats a bit cramped, and the danger of hypoxia was acute if the plane ever lost cabin pressure at altitude. But no transportation on earth held such prestige. If you looked out the window at ten or eleven miles above Iceland or the mid-Atlantic, you beheld amazing sights: the curvature of the earth, a thin layer of sky so blue it was cobalt, and above it the blackness of space.

Built and designed by Aérospatiale in France and by the British Aircraft Corporation, Concorde symbolized European pride and even ascendancy. Seats weren't cheap; in 1991, published prices for a New York–London round-trip were ten thousand dollars. The Ryder Cup party of forty got a nice discount from British Airways but it was still pricey. No matter—the British Professional Golf Association had recently come into some money. An antique it co-owned with the PGA of America and the European PGA Tour, a snoozer of an all-star match for golf professionals called the Ryder Cup, had suddenly become a worldwide roller-coaster ride and a matter of national pride. And valuable: Within a few years, between sales of logo shirts, corporate tents, tickets, and TV rights, the Cup would be making a $23 million profit on $63 million of revenue. The '91 Cup would clear roughly $10 million. Infighting over all that loot bubbled beneath the surface of the Ryder Cup's public tranquillity.

After climb-out, pretty flight attendants in form-fitting dresses with alternating vertical orange, white, and blue stripes patrolled the narrow blue-carpeted aisle. Smiling politely, they looked into the dark eyes of Severiano Ballesteros and the blue eyes of Colin Montgomerie and the haunted eyes of David Feherty and asked, "Would you care for some champagne, sir? Caviar?" They would. Beluga and bubbly were entirely appropriate for Europe's Ryder

Cup team. They were the kings of the golf world, and they were going in style at 1,350 miles per hour to kick America's ass. Again.

•

The history of the Ryder Cup contains many amusing twists and turns and memorable confrontations, but the condensed version looks like this: A workaholic chap from suburban London named Sam Ryder grew wealthy by packing seeds in little envelopes and posting them straight to the mail slots in the doors of the legions of English gardeners. "Everything from orchids to mustard and cress," was the catchy tagline of Heath and Heather Seed Company. Discovering leisure on doctor's orders, Ryder grew fond of golf and golf pros. He was also fond of being in charge, so when he instigated an international match in 1927 and donated an expensive gold cup, he put guidelines for the thing in writing. Rule One stipulated that the competition would be between teams of professionals from the United States and Great Britain. Strict adherence hurt England/Scotland/Wales over the years; when, for example, Henry Cotton left England for a job teaching golf in Belgium, he was not allowed on the team. This was a shame, because Henry was their stud. Furthermore, the United States had a larger population, a far better tour, and better players—Hagen, Hogan, Nelson, Snead—while Great Britain hosted a crippling home game called World War II.

So Team USA won year after boring year, and attention was not paid. But in 1979, Jack Nicklaus put the force of his personality and reputation behind rescinding Sam Ryder's prime directive. Ryder's daughter Joan agreed to amend the Deed of Trust to expand the Great Britain and Ireland side to include the best players from Continental Europe. In a few years, the Ryder Cup became competitive, then hysterically so.

Why all the emotion? Tabling the cultural and geopolitical explanations for the moment, we might focus on this simple equation: Losing what they had always won made the Americans more than a little *verklempt,* while winning what they had always lost put the European team and its supporters over the moon. Sam Torrance, he of the Groucho Marx mustache, personified the situation. The native of Largs, Scotland, hit the ball like Ben Hogan but putted like Hogan's grandma without her glasses. Then, in his eleventh year as a pro, Sam wiggled in enough putts to make the '85 Ryder Cup team. Endurance was his greatest strength: He rarely missed a European Tour event or his turn to buy the next round. Or, as the London *Evening Standard* reported chastely in a flattering bio, "He's a regular fixture in after competition drinking circles." Everyman Sam became a hero when he birdied the eighteenth hole in his singles match in '85, his fifteen-footer taking down Andy North and winning the Cup for Europe/GBI for the first time in twenty-eight years. A very joyous celebration ensued, with all the accoutrements of a war won: tears, man hugs, champagne spritzing, and group singing.

Torrance soon felt the other side of fame's sword. The tabloid press published details of the suddenly interesting man's split with his wife, including who slept with whom and where and why. On the other hand, his celebrity surely helped him land a smoking hot TV and film actress named Suzanne Danielle, who did not win an Oscar for her portrayals of Lola Pagola in the 1982 TV series *Jane* or for her Maria Sola in *The Trouble with Spies* (1987). Sam asked Danielle for her hand on the Concorde flight to the '87 Ryder Cup in Columbus, Ohio. She signaled affirmative. Captain Tony Jacklin got off a good line the night before the match began: "I'm resting you tomorrow, Sam. You're playing." Europe won again. Like fajitas being served at someone else's table, the celebration annoyed the other diners.

After losing all but four matches since '27 (there was one tie), Team Europe almost won in 1983; won in '85; won in '87; and tied in '89. The common denominators were Severiano Ballesteros, Torrance, Nick Faldo, Bernhard Langer, Ian Woosnam, and Captain Tony Jacklin. Perhaps Jacklin was the key. He had a chip on his shoulder as big as a wheel of cheese.

When Jacklin, then twenty-four, put in his first full campaign on the U.S. tour in 1968, an important faction of American players not only didn't like him, they let him know they didn't like him. "I have nothing whatsoever against foreign players coming over to America," wrote American pro Gardner Dickinson, who got everything off his chest in his 1994 book *Let 'er Rip!*. "Though I do think they should conduct themselves as guests, which they are." But Jacklin's plaid purple pants and ready smile contrasted with the banker's gray and grimness of Gardner and the other members of the American tour's old guard. The lad from Scunthorpe, England, won a few tournaments in the States, including the 1970 U.S. Open, which probably made the bad blood worse. "Jacklin's dress on the golf course was atrocious," wrote Dickinson. "He might as well have worn a big sign on his head imploring people to 'Look at me!'

"He despised Bob Goalby and me, and I do take pride in that. When Jacklin first came to the USA, he acted as if he were the great-grandson of George Washington instead of a guest, and, for the most part, he seemed to think he was doing our tour a favor when he played it . . . and nobody shed any tears when he went back home." Dickinson drew Jacklin in the singles in the '67 Ryder Cup match in Houston, and beat him, and counted it "one of the highlights of my career."

Jacklin sighed when recalling all this. "Goalby was a hard case," he said. "Gardner was bloody awful, mean-spirited. And Dan Sikes. . . . They resented you, like you were stealing their money." Jacklin reconciled with Goalby, and became close friends with American stars Nicklaus and Tom Weiskopf, but his appearances in the United States became increasingly rare—a sad self-exile for a player who was so good. After 1975 he never teed it up in another Masters, U.S. Open, or PGA, the major championships played in the United States.

Ultimately, the Ryder Cup brassed him off too. Jacklin's plastic BPGA-issued golf shoes literally fell apart during the '75 competition, an embarrassing reminder that the Americans draped themselves in cashmere and flew first class, while the British side sat in coach, in uniforms apparently supplied by the lowest bidder. The '77 Cup brought more humiliation. Captain Brian Huggett kept the savior of British golf on the bench for the final act, the singles, on Sunday. Jacklin objected, strenuously. This was at Royal Lytham, where he had won the '69

Open Championship. Insulting! When he was left off the 1981 team in favor of Mark James, Tony told the Ryder Cup to bugger off. He was through with it.

But then the world turned. At the behest of the BPGA, European Tour Director Ken Schofield invited Jacklin to lead the 1983 Ryder Cup team for its road match in Florida. "I'll want bloody Concorde," Tony said; he would not consider the job unless Team Europe had travel, equipment, and accommodation as luxe as the opposition enjoyed. Done. "And wives or girlfriends come along." Done. "Caddies too." Done.

Schofield and Jacklin agreed they'd have to get Seve back on the team; he didn't play in '81. There had been a dispute: Seve wanted to accept appearance money—cash for showing up at tournaments that wanted Señor Charisma very badly—while the administration was trying to stamp out the practice, which was hurting the feelings of those who weren't being offered a guarantee. Jacklin spoke soothingly to Seve over *huevos* at Royal Birkdale during the '83 Open. He described his own problems with the golf bureaucracy, and reminded his reluctant amigo that he had also been highly insulted at not being invited to the '81 Cup. Tony accepted the captaincy, and Ballesteros accepted his place on the team. Now with some very sharp arrows in his quiver, Jacklin had the perfect weapon to settle old scores.

While Team Europe stuck with Jacklin as its leader between '83 and '89, the U.S. team turned over its captainship, employing a Mount Rushmore of Nicklaus, Trevino, Nicklaus again, and then Floyd. Trevino mailed it in, but Nicklaus charged into the fray. Wadkins recalls with amazement that when he lost a spike on the battlefield, the greatest player in history dug around in an emergency bag he carried. Jack produced a spike and a wrench and fixed Lanny's shoe like a farrier. Unlike Lee, Jack had a jock background—basketball as a good high school player, and Ohio State football as a very big fan—so he knew what coaches do. He encouraged, cajoled, inspired when possible, and then he stepped aside. Jack downplayed what he did, saying it mostly consisted of "filling out the lineups and then standing around trying to look important."

But Jacklin outdid every captain ever by making almost a full-time job of promoting the Cup and pumping up his team. Not the first time he thumped a tub. To earn money to buy clubs and balls, ten-year-old Tony sold newspapers after school—loudly—outside the local steelworks to whom he remembered as the "gray-looking men" who trudged out of the mill. On Saturdays, he reported to another job he liked much better—assisting a man who purveyed woven goods from a booth at the outdoor market in his gritty little town in North Lincolnshire, England. "Tea cozies! Who can resist, a real bargain at three for one pound ten!" the man called out like a carnival barker. During the intervals when the boss left to wet his whistle at a nearby pub, Tony took over the selling.

Europe wouldn't have Jacklin at the helm this time around; Bernard Gallacher, himself a durable Ryder Cup player and Tony's assistant in the three matches from '85 to '89, was the new captain. Bernard (pronounced "burn-urd" if you please) and wife, Lesley, sat up front in Concorde. Both were from England. Across the aisle sat the magnificent Seve, the charismatic man from Basque Spain. Immediately behind them were Nick and Gill (England) and the teacup-sized Ian Woosnam and his equally miniature wife, Glendryth (Wales). Behind the Welsh rarebits sat David Feherty (Northern Ireland), his wife, Caroline (South Africa), and their son, Shey. Further along in the polyglot group were the recently widowed Jacklin; Carmen Ballesteros with his pacifier-sucking son, Baldomero; Colin Montgomerie and his beautiful new bride, Eimear, both from Scotland; and José María Olazábal (Spain), who had brought his mother.

Three members of the team would arrive from other parts of the globe. German Bernhard (pronounced "bairn-heart") Langer had been playing in Japan (Seve let it be known that he did not approve of this strenuous outing so close to the Ryder Cup and so far from South Carolina). And Sam Torrance was showing Paul Broadhurst (Northern Ireland) the sights and sounds of Endicott, New York. They held the B.C. Open there; Broadhurst had never played in the United States before and wanted a rehearsal before taking the stage at the Ryder Cup, which would be by several orders of magnitude the biggest thing ever in his life.

Paul impressed his impressively named girlfriend Jill Pickup by bringing her along on this adventure. Part of what made the Ryder Cup such a special occasion was the presence of the women. Wives and squeezes rarely traveled with their men on the European tour; there just wasn't enough money in it to support that as a business model.[1] The men without mates were naturally a collegial bunch, likely to dine and drink with one another in the one hotel at which the tour had reserved discounted rooms.

Common backgrounds united them further. Of the twelve men on Europe's '91 Ryder Cup team, only one, Montgomerie, had pursued education after high school, matriculating at Houston Baptist. Mark James likewise played a few years of amateur golf in his late teens and early twenties, but all the other Euro Cuppers got on with it. Jacklin and Langer had turned pro at fifteen; Seve at sixteen; Feherty and Torrance at seventeen; Captain Gallacher at eighteen; Faldo began to play for pay at nineteen; Olazábal turned pro at twenty.

The night before the flight, the confident defending champions coalesced at the posh Edwardian Hotel near Heathrow—that is, eight of them did. Seve and Carmen would be flying in from Madrid in the morning, and there were the three playing warm-up tournaments in the United States and Japan. Over pints in the dim light and polished copper of the Bijou Bar, golf's royalty discussed this and that, and someone asked David Gilford why he wasn't playing at the B.C. Open as he'd planned. "Couldn't get in," the mild-mannered Gilford replied. Couldn't get in? Rubbish. The U.S. Tour couldn't find a place for a Ryder

1 They played for a lot less in Europe. Due in part to a weak pound, Scotland's Sandy Lyle, the leading money winner in 1985, won the dollar equivalent of only $170,000 compared to the $542,000 won by the U.S. leader, Curtis Strange. The total prize money available on the European PGA Tour in 1990 was £16,100,425—about $26 million—versus $46 million on the PGA Tour.

Cup player? Couldn't get Bunky Henry or Gary McCord to stand aside?

Montgomerie tossed and turned all night. In the morning, the hubbub of fans and media in the airport terminal lit up his cerebral cortex like a flash grenade. Monty was one of the five rookies on the European team and he expected a lot of commotion, but he hadn't expected *this*. "Bloody hell," he whispered to Eimear. "We haven't even left the country yet."

Faldo added to the kerfuffle. In the glare of TV lights, the handsome Open and Masters champion issued the athlete's classic precompetition complaint: He perceived a lack of respect from the opponent. As bulletin board material it wasn't much, but it would do. Captain Dave Stockton responded the next day, Captain Bernard Gallacher responded to the response, and the writers had a new hook on which to hang a preview story. One of the other main themes was that no one on Team Europe except Torrance had ever even seen the Ocean. Did this indicate confidence—or overconfidence? Neither, said Gallacher, who spoke to the foreign journalists as if he were addressing a particularly dull set of second-graders. Europe is very far away from South Carolina, he said. Not that convenient to drop in. Our team wasn't finalized until a month ago. Do you understand?

"I have always been suspicious of the press," Gallacher admitted later. "So many journalists are not really interested in covering the golf but are always looking for an angle." Reticence would be his byword at Kiawah; he was a spokesman who did not wish to speak. A rumor riffled through the English tabloids and broadsheets that Seve had staged a stealthy coup d'état and taken control of the team.

The jet whispered through the high thin air and there was no turbulence. As it reached and exceeded the speed of sound, Concorde stretched by a foot. In high-speed turns, the fuselage flexed so much that passengers in the back could look toward the front and see the bend.

The mantislike Concorde entered North American airspace over Nova Scotia, then turned south, descending gradually over New England before landing in New York for refueling. Just a short distance from the Charleston airport, at a little after two P.M. local time, Captain Gallacher requested a flyover of Kiawah Island and the Ocean Course. The ship's captain readily agreed—he and everyone else on the crew were eager to please, having won a lottery for the honor of taking Europe's finest on this trip. The pilot dipped his wing this way, then that, while making wide, low circles over the ragged, subtropical coastline. The jet's engines were famously loud at low altitude. People on the ground on Kiawah, Seabrook, James, Daniel, and Johns islands looked up and gaped at the airship, so white against the gray sky. The airborne players, caddies, and fans huddled around Concorde's tiny windows. Kiawah gave little impression of an island from above—it was more like a peninsula, with only the skinny Kiawah River separating it from the mainland. But look how close the Ocean Course was to the ocean! It was practically in it! Strips of green fairway in two long rows laid on a spit of white sand.

After the flyby, the pilot flipped the toggle to lower the landing gear. No go. A wheel was stuck. The golfers, coaches, significant others, and about two-score of wealthy supporters endured a few minutes of anxiety as the jet continued to circle. A member of the flight crew lifted the carpet and forced the gear down manually. The wheel held. About 250 people inside the airport and thousands more around its perimeter watched the puff of smoke off the Michelins as the plane landed. Some had dressed in flag motifs to greet the great men, but many others were merely curious to see that wonder of the air, Concorde. The high whine of the Rolls-Royce/Snecma Olympus 593 engines softened to a whistle, then stopped. The players stood, looking smart in their matching Oscar Jacobson suits and ties. The jet bridge didn't fit, so they had to descend onto the runway, like so many rock stars or presidents.

2

FRIDAY, SEPTEMBER 22, 1989

Tropical Depression Eleven began on September 9 as a bit of unease in the warm air and water off the coast of West Africa. As Eleven gained wind speed and size, it moved up the ranks in the weather service designation, from Disturbance to Depression to Storm to Hurricane. It was a big one. Hurricane Hugo motored rapidly west toward Caribbean islands that sounded like the locales for a *Sports Illustrated* swimsuit shoot: Guadeloupe, Montserrat, Vieques. Banana crops were flattened, houses were flooded or blown over (or both), and several dozen people died.[1] The giant storm lost power after it slammed San Juan, but then reorganized as it continued north toward the U.S. mainland. It was as if Sherman's army was coming on the wind: Savannah

1 On St. Croix in the U.S. Virgin Islands, the island's only Olympic-size pool was destroyed; a local swimming phenom named Timothy Duncan feared working out in the ocean because of sharks, so in the coming months he would turn, reluctantly, to basketball.

evacuated, and Charleston-area residents got in the car and headed inland up I-26 toward Columbia.

Thirteen months before, late in the summer of 1988, the PGA of America had announced that the 1991 Ryder Cup would be contested on a still-to-be-built course on Kiawah Island. Hosannas echoed throughout the Low Country for the honor of the thing and for its economic impact, predicted to be about $19 million. After a permitting process made extra-long because of the environmental sensitivity of the Carolina coast, architect/builder Pete Dye didn't get started on the big dig until almost a year later, in July of '89. Dye and his wife/co-designer Alice moved into a house on Osprey Point, one of the three courses already in the ground at Kiawah. Then the worst hurricane in decades hit. The timing held a bizarre coincidence: On the very weekend that the '89 Ryder Cup was being played in England, Hugo attempted to wipe the host of the '91 Ryder Cup off the map. Everyone from Myrtle Beach to Beaufort would have been watching golf on TV if they hadn't been busy trying to stay alive.

Hugo knocked hard on the door on Thursday night and blew it in at four the next morning. The center of the fierce hurricane made landfall at Isle of Palms, a Charleston suburb just up the coast from Kiawah. "I'd been married six months," recalls Tommy Braswell, the golf writer for the Charleston *Post and Courier.* He shooed his wife off to stay with his mother in Charlotte, while he remained to protect home and hearth, and to observe. What he saw, he'll never forget: "I had a seventeen-foot Boston Whaler in my backyard, so I called my insurance agent to see what I should do besides put a tarp over it. He said I was OK."

He wasn't. Two giant loblollies breached the Braswell roof that night, and the boat (fiberglass hull, center console, outboard motor) just plain blew away. At the end of the ensuing long days of helping friends clean up and trying to keep a blue plastic cover on his house, Braswell dipped a five-gallon bucket into the sort-of clean water in his neighbor's pool, soaped up, and dipped again for a rinse. Everything about life in those days and weeks was disorienting: Coastal roads had disappeared under tons of sand; important bridges like the Limehouse and the Ben Sawyer could no longer carry a car; and hundreds of boats much bigger than Braswell's were deposited by the twenty-foot storm surge onto dry land far, far from their docks. It got hot; there was no electricity for air conditioning; some of Braswell's neighbors were without power for three weeks.

Someone estimated that there were about three thousand tornadoes embedded within Hugo. From the denuded look of a heretofore heavily wooded golf course in Mount Pleasant called Snee Farm, that seemed possible. The beach washed up on Wild Dunes, a new course on Isle of Palms; it would not reopen for almost a year.

Hugo also unraveled three months of prep work on the Ryder Cup venue at Kiawah Island. Marking stakes were God-knows-where, graded areas seemed never to have been touched by a dozer's heavy blade and treads, and thousands of fallen trees and closed roads and bridges blocked access and egress. About forty thousand pines had been uprooted, making the palm trees on the island more prominent. It was as if the thirteen-square-mile island had reverted to the 1670s—the beginning of the end of the Kiawah Indians.

The tribe had lived in the area for eons—possibly for as long as four thousand years, according to archaeologists. But late in the seventeenth century, an aggressive rival tribe called the Yuchi began kidnapping and enslaving Kiawahs. It got worse; entrepreneurs and settlers from Charles Towne came calling like so many siding salesmen. The recently emigrated English wanted the land and were annoying about it; a rebellion against them in 1674 did not go well for the natives. Thereafter, the offers to "sell" to the white men took on some urgency. We picture the Kiawahs in council in their round, bent-pole houses. They murmur about being under attack from two sides. The men wear loincloths. The women wear their hair long. Both genders have tattoos on their faces. . . . What could they do? For cloth, tools, and trinkets, they sold out and moved away. Between assimilation and European disease, the Kiawahs were extinct as a tribe by 1750.

Cattle would be just the thing for this little island, the new owners decided, roast beef for Charles Towne's Yorkshire pudding. Like a hurricane without a name, three hundred African slaves felled thousands of oaks, pines, and palms for pastures.

The highlight in the chain of custody in the ensuing centuries occurred in 1974, when the Kuwait Investment Company (KIC) paid $17,385,000 for Kiawah. Their big idea: a resort, such as the one succeeding down the coast at Hilton Head Island. The oil-rich gentlemen from the Middle East evicted twenty-five hundred free-range pigs and twenty wild horses while inviting in real estate, marketing, and construction pros from the Sea Pines Corporation, the group that had made such a success at Hilton Head. Kiawah Island Resort opened in May

'76 with a lovely inn with an ocean view; a beachside bar ideal for sunset watching and piña colada sipping; a shopping area called the Straw Market; seven green clay tennis courts and two made of concrete; and a Gary Player–designed golf course, called Marsh (later Cougar) Point.

"There was resistance at first about Kuwaitis owning Kiawah, especially from the Jewish community in Charleston," recalls Roy Barth, the resort's head tennis professional since day one. "Visions of camels and people in turbans, I guess. But they opened Beachwalker Park to the public, and that helped defuse the problem.

"Khalid Al Zouman was their representative here, a young man in his early thirties, educated at, I think, Ohio State. He could be pretty ruthless. I remember a meeting where each department head was told to cut fifteen percent from his budget in one week or resign."

Kiawah under Kuwait moved forward, but not at a breakneck pace. Perhaps the new owners were uncomfortable with spending so much on infrastructure, overhead, and golf courses. It wasn't like back home. In the liquid gold mine of the Rumaila oil field, on the border with Iraq, you picked a spot, punched a hole, ran a pipe, and the money flowed.

But here? Problems. For four years KIC tried to get the necessary approvals for a marina and adjacent housing. For four years, it failed. While environmentalists and politicians bloviated about dartfish and oyster beds, Seabrook, an adjacent island resort, got the approvals it needed to build a similar marina complex.

"Great dissatisfaction" developed regarding Kiawah, according to Abdulla Yaccoub Bishara, an influential Kuwaiti who had been president of the UN Security Council in 1979. Back home, he said, "They think it's a waste of money to invest in this island."[2]

In 1988, KIC sold out to KRA—Kiawah Resort Association, a small group of Charleston businessmen. KRA mitigated its cost by spinning off Kiawah's three golf courses and the ground for a proposed fourth. The buyer was residential real estate developer Landmark Land.

Landmark already had a deal in place with the PGA of America to host the '91 Ryder Cup at PGA West, a course it owned in southern California. It was going to be awesome, to use Dave Stockton's favorite word. PGA West was so infuriatingly difficult that after it hosted one of the rounds in the 1987 Bob Hope Chrysler Classic, PGA Tour pros circulated a petition—which passed—to never have the Hope there again. One of the bunkers was eighteen feet below the adjacent green! A man named Peter Dye had designed and built the place. The pros cursed his name.

After Landmark acquired the Kiawah golf courses, the company's principals cleared their throats and asked for attention. Changed our minds, they said. We shall conduct the '91 Ryder Cup on Kiawah Island, on what will be called the Ocean

2 We imagine the Kuwaitis in council in Kuwait City at the fortress-like palace of Emir Jaber III Al-Ahmad Al-Jaber Al-Sabah. Some of the men wear western business suits, some wear robes. Out the window are views of the Persian Gulf. "Al," someone says in Standard Modern Arabic, "let's just sell this stinker."

Course, which exists only on some maps and drawings and in the mind of Pete Dye.

This was shocking news. A brand new course would host the most anticipated tournament *ever*? Why the switcheroo? We want to make it easier for European TV viewers, explained Landmark and the PGA of America. A show emanating from the Eastern Time Zone instead of from the Pacific would be much more convenient for the sleep/wake cycles of Barcelonians and Edinburghers. But no one said the obvious: Interest in the '91 Ryder Cup was so high that instant fame and popularity would accrue to its host. And that's exactly what happened.

Landmark's key executives were ex-touring pros Joe Walser Jr., Ernie Vossler, and Johnny Pott. They believed as an article of faith that a memorable, high-end golf course spurred lot sales around it, so it was no surprise that they had been drawn to the feisty Dye, the seat-of-his-pants designer from Indiana. Pete could do memorable, that was certain, but his restless desire to make the ground he shaped *just so* often caused him to tinker up to and past his deadline. He would agree to a change—a larger green, the removal of a tree—and then not do it. Other architects delivered a set of plans and drainage and irrigation schemes and then stood back, but Dye stayed on-site and got his hands dirty, and he casually ignored what the draftsmen put on paper. He'd spend hours alone, gazing at a piece of ground, then mount a D2 Caterpillar Dozer and regrade a fairway, sculpt a green or a tee, or improvise a set of bunkers. In other words, Pete could be infuriating to work with until his client learned to just leave him alone. He had his vision, and it wasn't subject to debate.

"Pete Dye is a genius with a flat piece of ground, maybe any piece of ground," says Dick Youngscap, who hired Dye to make something out of 270 acres of Nebraska. "Pete decided we needed thirty-five more acres, so we got it, but it wasn't easy. . . . We're walking in a grove of trees one day and Pete says, 'Here's a great par three for ya, Dick.' I couldn't see anything but the trees." Firethorn Golf Club in Lincoln opened in 1986 and was an immediate and enduring hit.

In 1963, not long after they hung out their shingle, Pete and Alice had traveled to Scotland to study the Old Masters and their masterpieces—Turnberry, Prestwick, Royal Dornoch, Carnoustie, the Old Course. "We had imprinted on our minds," Dye later wrote, "a type of design that was straightforward and honest and difficult as hell." Tour players moaned about the Dyes' modern interpretation of the classics, but his designs ascended to golf course heaven because they hosted the biggest tournaments. Dye did Oak Tree in Edmond, Oklahoma, for Landmark (they held the 1988 PGA Championship there). A month before the Ryder Cup, the PGA Championship of '91 would be contested on another Dye design, Crooked Stick, in Indiana; and his Harbour Town, on Hilton Head Island, held an annual Tour event. The Dye-designed Stadium Course at TPC Sawgrass in Ponte Vedra Beach, Florida, included the new most famous hole in golf, the island green seventeenth, and it was the permanent home of the Players Championship—probably the fifth biggest annual event in golf, a notch behind the majors. Lots always sold briskly near where Pete dug.

The Stadium was the antecedent of the Ocean. Before Dye got ahold of them, both were sandy, swampy tropical paradises for alligators, snakes, deer, egrets, and a thousand other creatures. As he built the Stadium in 1981, Dye did things to swamps he'd never get away with again. He drained 'em, dug 'em out, changed their outlines, and piped their water and tiny critters into lagoons. In the ensuing years, swamps and marshes were rebranded "wetlands" to upgrade their prestige and to facilitate the passage of more and tougher laws to protect their delicate and complicated ecosystems. The Environmental Protection Agency, the South Carolina Coastal Council, and the South Carolina Coastal Conservation League leaned in close as plans for the Ocean Course were introduced and amended.

The proposed track was long and skinny, with two parallel nines in the pattern of a very long figure eight. Vast wetlands reposed on the inland side and a long, continuous dune on the ocean side. When Hugo blew in like an almighty hammer only a couple of months into construction, the high, two-mile-long sand dune got broken up, flattened out, and stripped bare. Gorgeous ancient oak trees lay on their sides. No one could get on or off the island except by boat.

"Hugo made it *easier* to build the Ocean Course," says George Frye, the director of golf maintenance at Kiawah when the Dyes moved in. It was Frye's job to grow grass on the substrate Dye created. "We only had a general permit. Pete went out and did what he wanted. No one had time to worry about what was going on at the Ocean Course. This whole county was torn all to hell."

With no one telling him not to, Dye created his own dunes and lagoons, pushed and dug the silty sand the way he saw fit, and devised an ingenious system of underground basins that caught and recirculated the water and chemicals used on the course, thus preventing any wetland contamination. His right-hand man, Jason McCoy, came up with a way to restore vegetation to the denuded dunes. By injecting water and fertilizer directly into the mounds of sand, sea oats and beach grass were successfully transplanted en masse for the first time. It wasn't that Dye was a poor steward of the environment, and the weeks of working at night were not necessarily indications of skullduggery. He was just a man on a mission, with a very big clock ticking, and input from well-meaning bureaucrats would have only slowed him down.

3

THURSDAY, APRIL 18, 1991

The course was too hard.

A touring professional from North Carolina named Charles Henry Beck missed the cut at the Masters, then, by special dispensation, got to play a practice round at the still unopened Ocean Course. The day was unseasonably warm and unsettled. The playful wind blew hard, then soft, hard, then soft. Pete Dye's playground looked raw: Two weeks before resort guests could pay a green fee and tee it up, the transplanted sea oats had not taken hold, the fairway grass had not grown in, and straw strewn on the dunes to prevent movement and erosion gave an under-construction look to everything. Were those street sweepers parked over there? They were: So much beach sand was blowing onto the course that the club had had to take it up with a couple of big Tennant machines capable of cleaning Fifth Avenue.

Following a stellar year in which he had finished tied for eighth in the Masters and tied for second in the U.S. Open, Chip Beck had been the best American player in the '89 Ryder

Cup. He and Paul Azinger won two out of two, taking down the heretofore invincible team of Faldo and Woosnam; in singles, Beck beat Bernhard Langer, which was just as impressive. Everyone on the U.S. side wanted Chip to play in the grudge match at Kiawah, and Chip badly wanted to play. He was a thoroughly likable and sincere man with a future, as it turned out, in insurance sales. But his golf game ebbed and flowed like the ocean, and at the moment the tide was out. He was not playing badly, exactly, but not doing well enough to make an all-star team. In six weeks, he'd miss the cut at the next big event, the U.S. Open. Two majors, two missed cuts . . . potential Ryder Cuppers were being watched like critical-care patients, and not all of them were thriving. But here he was at Kiawah, full of hope.

"He'd hit one slightly off-line, and the wind would take it, and it would hit the side of the green and bounce away," recalls Jeremy Colie, who did every golf-related job at the Ocean Course—driving range, club storage, carts—including caddying for Chip Beck. "Then the same thing would happen at the next hole, and the next. I think he began to feel a little overmatched. When we got rained out after ten holes, he looked relieved."

The course was too hard.

4

WEDNESDAY, SEPTEMBER 18, 1991

"Hey, Larry! What's up?" Eight days before the start of the Cup, Boston Celtics forward Larry Bird and one of his four brothers teed it up at the Ocean Course. A nearby foursome called and waved, not making a big deal out of it. They were stars too.

And they were goofballs. Paul Azinger proved it by loosening the clasps on the straps holding Payne Stewart's bag on his cart, so that his pal's red-and-white Wilson Staff golf bag crashed to the ground as he accelerated his Club Car golf cart. He did the same thing to Corey Pavin, giving the little man's wood driver a serious case of cart-path rash. In another gambit, Paul sneaked ice chips onto the seat where Payne sat; the ice did what it does in warm sun, and Stewart had to endure wet shorts. Trash was talked, and fart bombs exploded at the tops of backswings. The most effective needler in the group was Mark Calcavecchia, who had learned from masters, his older brothers. Calc looked like a high school football lineman twelve years past his use-by date. Stewart might have been the golden-haired quarterback who dated a cheerleader (in fact, he had been) and Azinger was a still-in-shape free safety ready to hit someone. The fourth member of the group, Corey Pavin, seemed wispy and insubstantial next to these big lugs.

They played ten-dollar skins and wore Bermuda shorts and sunscreen. Ken Burger, the executive sports editor of the Charleston *Post and Courier*, watched with something close to amazement. These were not the stone-faced pros he'd seen on television. "They race each other down the fairways in their golf carts," he wrote. "Or use them like bumper cars or fishtail them down the sandy cart paths trying to throw dust in each other's eyes." The nearby beach and the serpentine trails around the sand dunes at the Ocean Course seemed to bring out the kids in them.

Goofy Stewart wrung the fun out of life as if it were water in a towel. He'd majored in beer at Southern Methodist University, played the minor league Asian tour, met an Australian girl in Malaysia and married her, and had innumerable comic adventures in Thailand, Indonesia, and Korea. Through diligent practice, he had become a Zen Master of the Handy Gasser, a handheld fart machine—great for taxis, elevators, and the moment when a nervous CEO was about to hit his first shot in a pro-am.

At the hotel at the Belfry in '89, Stewart woke his teammates each morning by blasting "Born in the U.S.A." or "We Are the Champions" on his boom box. Lanny Wadkins recalled the time he and some other pros staggered out of a plane from Tokyo and sleepwalked through customs in LAX or SFO at five in the morning. "Around the corner comes Payne, eating a foot-long chili cheese dog with onions. Most disgusting thing you've ever seen. 'Come on, guys, it's great!' he says. And damned if we all didn't get one."

Stewart required the spotlight the way peacocks require peahens. He played harmonica in Peter Jacobsen's pickup band, and he played the fop each time he stepped between the ropes. His plus twos and the shiny metal toes on his shoes were impossible to miss in a fashion era of khaki pants and logoed gimme caps. At the 1987 Masters, Stewart wore pale pink knickers, pink polka-dotted knee socks, a white dress shirt, and a pink bow tie. Yellow metal tips on the white shoes, and a tam—not a Wilson billboard—on his handsome head.

What explained his look-at-me style? Possibly he understood what most of his peers could not fathom, that they were all in the entertainment industry. Maybe it was an acute case of vanity, linked with a desire to sell Payne Stewart brand clothing. Or was it his childhood? As the youngest of three, and the only boy, Payne had bathed in attention and affirmation like it was bathwater. His sisters and mother doted on *le petit prince*, and his father felt so involved that he once got a technical foul—from the stands—so loudly did he berate the referees in one of his son's basketball games. Payne was the quarterback, the point guard, and, of course, a hell of a golfer. He was a gum chewer, and cocky as hell.

Some aspects of Payne weren't so goofy, though. His aggressive sense of humor, for one thing, is described by a friend as "caustic . . . it rubbed a lot of people the wrong way." He was willing to put in the hours on the practice tee. His instructor,

Chuck Cook, knew without a doctor's diagnosis that this was a student who couldn't focus on the humdrum. Hit a hundred five irons? No way. "Payne was particularly good at difficult things, like shots from a downhill lie out of a divot, or pitches with a towel as a target," Cook says. "This appealed to his ADD. And he was totally nonanalytical. He'd have a shot with the ball below his feet, and he'd say, 'Hey, Chuck. Which way is this supposed to go—right or left? I always forget.' "

Stewart became an increasingly vocal Christian, but sometimes his religiosity sounded self-serving and puerile, or like just another game-improvement strategy. At the 1989 PGA Championship—which he won—Stewart told the press his thoughts while watching from the scorer's tent as the last player who could tie him holed out. "I said a prayer in the tent," Stewart said. " 'How about some good stuff for Payne Stewart?' He obliged me by letting me win."

After the fallout from that and a few other attacks of thoughtless candor, Payne became a tough interview. He and his wife, Tracey, came to view writers as a lurking enemy rather than a source of credible free publicity. "He literally pushed me aside by the eighteenth green at the Belfry in '93," recalls *Golf World* executive editor Ron Sirak. "But later he apologized—twice—for having been a jerk. I thought he was trying to be a nicer guy."

Stewart would be making his third consecutive Ryder Cup appearance. He had won two and lost two in the debacle at Muirfield Village in '87, where he had been part of the only U.S. Ryder Cup squad not to march out with the opposing team for the final ceremony, because Captain Jack Nicklaus had sequestered them in his house for a bawling out. "Look at you, Payne Stewart," Jack had said. "You win all this money, but how many tournaments have you won?" The answer, to that point, was five. During the tie of '89 in England, Payne had won his first match with Wadkins as his partner (everyone won with Lanny) but then the beknickered man lost three in a row. The disappointments ignited Stewart's Ryder Cup fever as wins never could, and he fretted to his wife early in '91 that the sore neck that was keeping him out of the winners circle would also keep him off America's team. But then he won the U.S. Open at Hazeltine, solving both problems.

•

Payne's bag crashed to the sandy ground, damaging the head of his driver. Azinger giggled and sped away. With a grip as strong as garlic breath and a swing arc that described a hockey player's slap shot, Azinger hit hooks. Hooks roll. On the 543-yard second hole at the Ocean Course, Zinger crunched a driver and his three wood[1] onto and over the green, but he thinned his third from a sand dune past the target again, a hacker's shot. "I didn't want to take any sand," Azinger said. "I didn't want the environmentalists coming after me."

That small joke hinted at a key to his personality, the way he looked for and found conflict. In that sense, a life of weekly competition in golf tournaments—not to mention Ryder

1 Azinger had helped start an equipment company, called Hurricane; his metal three wood had been named Hugo.

Cups—was perfect for him. The purity of his competitive fire was fun to watch and made him easy to root for. His joy at drilling practice balls at the poor schmo driving the range picker and his delight at messing with Payne was all of a piece: Azinger stayed on the lookout for opposing forces.

Perhaps his us-versus-them worldview originated with his father, Ralph, a my-way-or-the-highway patriarch who flew combat missions in Vietnam. Like Stewart a Scripture-quoting Christian, Azinger rued what he called in his 1995 autobiography the "secular humanism and evolution" they'd taught him in high school in Florida. In *Zinger*, one of his twenty-four celebrity blurbers was right-wing radio commentator Rush Limbaugh. "Paul Azinger exemplifies the natural qualities of leadership that arise from a strong moral foundation," wrote Rush.

There had been no eye-opening or world-expanding overseas apprenticeship for Paul; he and wife Toni lived in and traveled these United States in a silver-and-orange Vogue camper for three years in the early eighties. He had a gun and a fishing pole and he often caught dinner, and they were happy. He took his first trip abroad when he was twenty-seven, to play in the '87 Open Championship at Muirfield in Scotland, and damn near won.

Azinger's low-ball style and clever strategizing seemed made for the game Over There, and he was in or near the lead the whole way. In Saturday's third round, he battled the course and the cold, blowing rain in the company of Nick Faldo, whom he had never heard of, and who didn't speak a word all day. In the final round, with a three-shot lead and nine holes to play, Azinger bogeyed eleven and twelve, while ahead of him the unusually self-involved Faldo made par after par. And par after par: Nick, nicknamed Fold-o by the cruel British press for his history of coming close, made what they call "standard figures" on all eighteen holes. When Paul bogeyed seventeen and eighteen, the par machine had won by one.

"I enjoyed being center stage here," Azinger said in the aftermath. "I love the thought of the whole world watching me. If you're afraid of the center stage in this game, you're nothing." After the torture of the awards ceremony—as runner-up with Rodger Davis, Zinger had to remain—the happy Faldo and the devastated Azinger exchanged their first-ever words. "Sorry about that," Nick said.

Paul didn't like the tone; he inferred condescension and insincerity. Since he'd borne the pressure of leading the tournament most of the week, he felt he deserved more or better consolation from the new champion golfer for 1987. Later, the technically perfect Faldo belittled Azinger's "homemade grip and hatchet swing" to a journalist. The skinny Yank put the new Open champion on the list of guys he'd like to beat forevermore. First on that list, of course, was Seve.

Still brooding about his near miss in the British, Azinger played poorly at the next major, the PGA, which was notable for him only because it was the first time he was paired with the Spanish Sensation. "You no worry about this," Severiano Ballesteros said as they left their thirty-sixth hole together. "You are a very good player." To David Feherty's ear, Seve's Spanglish made a well-known expletive sound like "son off the beach."

Ten months later, Azinger and Ballesteros came together again in the tiny world at the top of professional golf when they were paired in the final round of the '88 U.S. Open at the Country Club in suburban Boston. Seve quick-hooked out-of-bounds on the first hole and appeared to resign himself to a down-the-list finish. Meanwhile, Azinger was making everything on the first nine to shoot a six-under-par 30, tying a Major record. Then from some deep-seated desire to inspire someone to win if he couldn't win himself, Seve began to coach and encourage Paul. "You need to make one more birdie, you win this tournament," he said. Then, after a bobble, "Is OK. You no worry about this. You need to birdie this hole."

The encouragement amazed and amused Azinger. "Anyone but Faldo, right?" he said to his coach for a day. At the end, Zinger's 66 got him a tie for sixth, three shots out of the Faldo/Strange play-off, which Curtis won.

The camaraderie disappeared at the '89 Ryder Cup. Now Seve whispered emphatic Castilian into the ear of José María Olazábal, who played Robin to his Batman, or, more on point, Bernardo to his Zorro. Their brand of Spanish turned the letters *C*, *S*, and *Z* into *TH*, making the word for five—*cinco*—sound like think-o. Zorro was Thor-o. The Spaniards steamrolled their American opponents in the team portion of the match, winning 3½ of a possible 4 points. Then Thor-o and Thing-er squared off in singles.

Azinger, desperate for a point for his desperate team, overreacted to advice from Curtis Strange, who had lost twice to Seve in '87 and once in the '89 match. "He prides himself on being a great match-play player. Don't let him pull anything on you," Curtis said. In Ballesteros vs. Azinger—the first match on Sunday morning—pressure filled the air like humidity. On the second hole, Seve made the most innocuous request, to be allowed to switch his damaged ball on the green. No one ever says no to this—but Azinger did. Seve couldn't believe it. "Is this the way you want to play today?" he asked. It was. Neither player gave the other a putt all day.

•

All felt in order for Zinger two years later, on the eve of the '91 Ryder Cup. He had just the right amount of animosity in his heart toward at least two-twelfths of the opposing team. And he felt better than he had in five years. In June, a surgeon had arthroscopically scraped away bone and scar tissue from his chronically aching right shoulder, and removed one of the bursae, nominally a little sac of lubricant, but possibly the cause of his pain. Azinger tried to play in the PGA Championship in August but he wasn't quite ready; his withdrawal cleared the way for an alternate named John Daly. Now, in the sand and sun at Kiawah, Paul's shoulder felt like new. But the little dark spot on the head of his humerus would turn out to be cancer. He wouldn't become aware of the spreading lymphoma for two more years.

Stewart, Azinger, and Calcavecchia hit cannon shots down the corridors between the dunes. Pavin fired his peashooter and hoped for some roll. But no one felt sorry for the little guy whose mustache and splay-footed walk channeled Charlie Chaplin, for he was kicking ass on the U.S. Tour. The little man—five foot nine in spikes, 150 pounds—was having the best financial year of anyone in golf. He would end 1991 having won two tournaments and a shade under $1 million—tops on the money list.

He played an old-school game, painting the golf course with cuts and punches and canny running shots. He may have been the best competitor of the four, maybe not, but without doubt he made the most out of the fewest physical gifts. Where was his head this sunny day? Again with the religion: only three months before, Pavin had renounced the Judaism he'd grown up in. Only days before, he'd been baptized into his wife's faith, Roman Catholicism. Eventually, he'd espouse a Protestant, evangelical, born-again theology, the same as Payne and Paul. At the next Ryder Cup, he and Bernhard Langer would lead a Sunday-morning prayer service on the eighteenth green at the Belfry.

"I felt a void in my life," Pavin said, and Christianity filled it. But if Jesus gave him the peace to play golf very, very well, there was also a price to pay. Jack Pavin, Corey's father, the owner of several shoe stores back home in Los Angeles, took his Jewishness seriously. He'd been president of a service organization called the Brotherhood at their Reform synagogue, Temple Beth Torah in Ventura, so when Corey left the faith of his father, the two had a falling out. A lot of Jews don't recognize even the possibility of conversion. On the other hand, a friend recalls how welcoming and supportive other Christians were to this particular convert. If Corey was in turmoil, he kept it to himself.

Pavin was a Ryder Cup rookie but was such a cool, tenacious

competitor that no one on the team worried about him. With his artistic short game and an absolute refusal to beat himself, Corey was someone you'd hate to face in match play.

Not so Calc.

Back in the dark days of the early eighties, Mark Calcavecchia had always traveled with his bowling ball. He called it his rock. The rock sat in a bag in the corner of the trunk of his yellow Camaro, nestled close to his white Ping staff bag. For a seeming eternity, the beer-barrel-chested pro from Nebraska roamed the United States, not playing well enough to make a living but unable to conceive of another career. Five times he got his PGA Tour card. Five times he lost it. He earned less than ninety thousand dollars total from '81 to '85—mere peanuts when you're living on the road. Nights found him ordering two Big Macs at the drive-through and taking them back to a hotel that wasn't the Ritz. He chewed the all-beef-patties-special-sauce-lettuce-cheese-pickles-onions-on-a-sesame-seed-bun, gripped and drained the contents of six cold aluminum cans, waved the remote at the TV. Some evenings he found a bar and drank some more. But other times, Big Mark obeyed the siren song of a heavy ball rolling on gleaming hardwood, the two- or three-second buildup, and then the controlled violence of sixteen pounds of hard plastic crashing into ten vase-shaped blocks of rock maple.

Calc grew up a kegler, and was good at it. With no practice, he maintained a 195 average, just five pins less than the minimum required to compete on the Pro Bowlers Association tour. Back home in tiny Laurel, in northeast Nebraska, his insurance agent father had made ends meet for Mark, his two older brothers, and wife Marjorie by managing Hillside Bowl, an eight-laner at Highway 20 and West Third. Bowling was something to do during the winter, but golf was John Calcavecchia's passion. He and a few friends scraped out nine holes in a cornfield and called it Cedar View Country Club. According to Marjorie, the little back-and-forth course became Mark's best friend.

The family moved to North Palm Beach when Mark was thirteen, on the theory that Florida sunshine would ease the pain of John's incipient multiple sclerosis. It helped, but not enough. As it became impossible for his father to swing a club, "I became his golf," Calc recalled. He won the junior tournaments every prodigy wins, enrolled at the University of Florida, discovered beer, and, he says, "never went to class." He dropped out at age twenty and turned pro. His awful diet resulted in weight gain and, probably, moodiness. Once he hit a drive he hated and slammed the offending club onto a cart path; its head flew off, nearly into the head of a woman spectator, whose husband raised hell. "I had to write a letter and I got fined up the ass," Calcavecchia told Cameron Morfit of *Golf* magazine. "Probably the worst thing I've ever done."

He also dealt with feelings of not belonging. "I'm in the wrong fucking game," he said after being paired with Andy Bean in Canada and watching the big redhead shoot 62. On putting greens and practice tees, Calcavecchia crept to the side to avoid being near golf's recognizable stars. But a simple grip change transformed his standard shot from a hook to a gentle fade and in '86 he won for the first time. Calc played instinctively, fearlessly, and his ability to perform golf's most useful trick shot—the lob—recalled his ability to pick up a 7-10 split.

He had power and a safecracker's touch. When he lobbed his way to a win in the '89 British Open—in a play-off with Australians Wayne Grady and Greg Norman—his credentials were secure.

Calcavecchia had won five times on the Tour by '91, six if you include his win at Royal Troon. But his uncanny knack of finishing second—twenty-seven times, eventually, the third most in the history of the PGA Tour—indicated a latent weakness. Sure, the other guy chipped in against him in play-offs sometimes, but it couldn't all be bad luck. In 1984, in the Tour's only big match play event, he built a seven-up lead over T. C. Chen with nine holes to play yet managed to lose. As for the Ryder Cup, he'd been 1-1 at Muirfield Village in '87, but the win was a tasty one, one-up over Faldo. In '89, he played in every match, and was 2-2 going into the final-day singles, but hit it into the lake on eighteen at the Belfry—twice. No choice but to concede the point to Ronan Rafferty of Ireland. Ronan celebrated, Mark wept.

But September of '91 was a good time to be Calc. He looked terrific. He'd been married in '87 to Sheryl, a hairdresser and aerobics instructor. She'd engineered a weight reduction from 230 to 200 and improved her man's coif. Nice threads too: He had a new deal with Italian manufacturer Fila. At the end of the day in this Ryder Cup practice round, the other guys paid him. He'd shot 64.

5

THURSDAY, SEPTEMBER 12, 1991

"Hey, Dale, you want to caddie for Freddie?" Two weeks before the Ryder Cup, three other members of the U.S. team came to Kiawah to introduce themselves to the Ocean Course. Ocean Course, meet Lanny, Raymond, and Fred.

It would be golf pros caddying for golf pros this day. Jim Kelcchi, an assistant pro at Marsh Point, had been informed that Wadkins, Floyd, and Couples were on their way: "I knew Dale liked Freddie, so I let him have first pick. I took Floyd. Lanny brought his own caddie."

Dale Mercer, then an assistant at Turtle Point on Kiawah, remembers an atmosphere that was purposeful but not tense. The gravity of the situation was underlined by the fact that there was no bet; unusual, because Wadkins and Floyd rarely deigned to hit a ball without a wager. Twenty-dollar one-downs were their standard game; when someone won a hole, a new bet started. "Fred was engaged, a super nice guy," Mercer recalls. "He was still hitting a persimmon driver, a Tommy Armour MacGregor 845, but he had that metal three-wood, a Ram, that he'd gotten out of Tom Watson's trunk. Belonged to Tom Watson's wife! I wasn't sure I'd like Lanny—the way he competed, I thought he was hard-edged, a tough guy. But he was sensational, very likable and a real gentleman. Floyd was all business."

Aim at that tree with a draw, Jim said. This green won't hold with this wind, Dale said. Can you believe what Jimmy Connors is doing at the U.S. [tennis] Open with that yellow racquet? someone said. What is he, forty? Jesus, this course is tough. I'd hate to have to play it for a score. . . . Ray or Lanny asked Fred if he was playing at the B.C. next week.

Yes, he was. Couples would travel to upstate New York to play in the B.C. Open the week before the Ryder Cup. He'd shoot 66-67-68-68, and win, ho-hum, by three over Peter Jacobsen. The frustrating game seemed to frustrate him less than anyone else who played for a living. His temperament bordered on inert. In '91 and '92, he would recall much later, "golf seemed really, really easy." He didn't seem even slightly reactive to pressure. His languid swing and walk made you want to guess at his pulse rate: Fifty beats per minute? Forty? During a delay at a college golf tournament—he played for the University of Houston—Couples lay down on a tee, tipped his visor over his eyes, and fell sound asleep.

With his thunderous drives booming off that solid block of old persimmon and pure striking with the other clubs, Couples did not endure a long tuition on the Tour. He turned pro right out of college, had two decent years, then won the Kemper

Open in his third. He'd grown up in Seattle, the son of a parks-and-rec employee who tended the grounds at the zoo. He was Italian on his father's side. A generation or two before, the family surname had been changed from Coppola.

"I've noticed that you cut the ball a little with your woods," observed Mercer midway through the round. "And you draw the irons. Why?"

Couples shrugged. "I don't know," he said.

Some found him enigmatic. He seemed possessed of talent but not of focus. He began sentences that wandered through the ether, searching in vain for a home. Often his statements contained strange inner truths, delivered in the oracular style of Yogi Berra or George W. Bush: "I'm not great, I'm good, and good's not bad," Fred said, and "I don't answer the phone because there might be someone on the other end." Women sighed at the callipygian curve in his pleated Ashworths, men loved his easy manner and major power off the tee, and both genders called his name apropos of nothing when he walked by. He hated it. He was, is, shy. He and the practice tee were not in a relationship. "Practice literally wore me out, even when I was in my twenties," he told Jaime Diaz of *Golf Digest*. "I don't have the mentality to go out there for two hours and get drenched in sweat."

Inevitably, he heard the u-word. Nicklaus found him to be the perfect example of a generation of underachievers, a talented group that simply did not burn to win. When Tom Weiskopf said something similar from the TV broadcast booth, he and Couples traded public insults.

Couples had played in one Ryder Cup—the previous one—

but not well. Captain Raymond Floyd gave his low-key rookie a place next to the high-key veteran Wadkins in the afternoon of the first day. Everyone won with Lanny. The opponents were Mark James ("he walks along the fairways as if in terminal despair," according to the scouting report in Malcolm Hamer's *The Ryder Cup: The Players*) and Howard Clark ("a powerful player with an uncertain temperament"). But Despair and Uncertain Temperament won 3 and 2. Shocked at this—how do you lose with Lanny?—Captain Floyd kept Fred on the bench until Sunday, a dark, dank day in central England. With the Match excruciatingly close and their singles match level on the final hole, Couples fired a howitzer, about seventy yards past his opponent's drive. Christy O'Connor Jr., who had sung "Danny Boy" at the closing dinner of his only other Ryder Cup, in '75, responded with the best shot of his life, a two-iron from 230 yards that stopped three and a half feet from the hole. "It was a dazzling thrust," wrote the excellent Hamer, "that so discountenanced Couples that he pushed his nine-iron shot weakly to the right." The Irishman won the hole and the match, and both men wept. At the closing ceremony, Fred wore dark glasses.

Now, two years later, Couples strolled the sunny Ocean Course, with the sounds of seagulls and breaking waves in his ears. He was thirty-one, almost thirty-two. So what was he doing with Wadkins, forty-one, and Floyd, forty-nine? This was psychological profiling by Captain Stockton. If Fred lacked fire, it seemed logical to expose him to two towering competitive infernos, and to make Ray and Fred a couple in the foursomes and fourballs. Floyd's perceived ability to inspire Freddie was the main reason he made the team, according to Lanny, instead of Tom Kite, who was not inspirational, and who had the yips besides. In November 1990, Ray 'n' Fred had been teammates in the Ronald McDonald Charity Classic, the precursor to the Shark Shootout, a silly-season event in California employing a mixture of best-ball and scramble formats. They shot a silly 182, *34 under* for 54 holes. Maybe Couples fired up Floyd.

The practice round continued. Because most of the fairways had been elevated by six feet—Alice Dye's idea—the ocean and its moods were visible on almost every hole. Bunkers blended into dunes that blended into beach that merged with the Atlantic. If you didn't watch yourself, you'd fall into reverie at the magnificence of the setting. But the challenge of the golf snapped you back. Like a two-hundred-acre *New York Times* crossword puzzle, the course presented a series of intriguing challenges that were sometimes just too damn much. What's a five-letter word for "I don't have this shot"? *Shank?* Like his patron saint, Alister MacKenzie (he read and referred to Mac's 1920 book *Golf Architecture* until his copy was dog-eared), Dye disguised safety at the Ocean Course. But Wadkins—Dye's opponent, in a way—was practically impossible to fool; he deciphered in an instant what was camouflage, and what was real danger. Golf's fastest player looked like he could break par on the back of a galloping polo pony; Lanny selected a stick and a vector without delay, then sent the ball away, usually pretty low. Altitude wasted time. Post-hit, he'd often lean on his club, oozing impatience. Is this the first four-iron you've ever hit? read the thought bubbles over his head. They paying you by the hour?

His stylistic opposite, Bernhard Langer, would be playing for Europe. Langer required long intervals of analysis and reflection to decide if he wanted a sweater or not, and he deliberated over picking a club or a line to the hole as if he were adjudicating a tax case. Pity Lanny if he had to play him again. The German tortoise had beaten the Virginia hare all four times they'd played in Ryder Cups.

With his scrunched-up backswing, his wristy slash of a downstroke, and a one-word game plan—*Attack*!—Wadkins resembled another Wake Forest alum: Arnold Palmer. Arnie was popular, to put it mildly, but shaking every hand and remembering every name didn't matter to Lanny. "How do you do," he'd say to four nervous amateurs on the first tee of the pro-am. "I'm Lanny Wadkins. I'm not looking for your ball." The quote is apocryphal, of course, but its durability revealed something about him. In the British press, the one-word adjective attached to his name was *combative.*

"Here comes this stocky, cocky little guy with a pudgy face and maybe a little belly, and more brass than you can haul around in a GMC pickup," wrote Rick Reilly in *Sports Illustrated* in June. The photo with the story was unforgettable: Lanny ironing a shirt. It turned out that wrinkled clothing made him crazy. If his pants got rumpled during breakfast at the hotel, he'd go back to the room and iron them flat again. And Reilly corrected the misperception that Wadkins disliked playing with amateurs. He didn't; he even played in the member-guest at his home club, Preston Trail, in Dallas. What he disliked was slowness. He and his younger brother Bobby, sons of a Richmond, Virginia, truck driver, learned to despise any delay that kept them from playing fifty-four holes on a summer day.

Lanny cried when he told his father he'd made the Walker Cup squad (he played on two of them). Team play turned him on. Look at his stats: His numbers on the PGA Tour peaked in odd years, ensuring he would be one of the elite twelve, which he was eight times, tied for the most ever.

"I just loved it," Wadkins says today. "I was a tough competitor. Sometimes I pissed people off. OK, a lot of times I pissed people off. On the Tour you're a lone wolf, ordering room service, and friendships don't last or only last a week. But in Ryder Cup you have people pulling for you. Being with the guys, becoming close friends with Calc and Payne and Ken Green, the competition, playing for your country . . . I loved all of it."

Beginning in 1977, one week out of every 104 the lone wolf became Jason Kidd—which is to say, the assist leader, the selfless teammate setting up scores for others. You can make this putt, Lanny would say, I *know* you can. "I meshed well with Hale [Irwin], Larry Nelson, OK with Payne and Raymond, good with Stadler and Fuzzy [Zoeller]. Ed Sneed and I played great together. [But] Kite and I were oil and water, it just didn't work."

In U.S. Ryder Cup history, Wadkins and Palmer are tied for most fourball matches won (nine), and most foursomes matches won (seven). Only Arnie has won more total matches (twenty-two to twenty) and only Billy Casper and Arnie scored more Ryder Cup points (23½ and 23 to Lanny's 21). But Palmer, Casper, Demaret, Burke, Snead, and the other American pros with gaudy numbers played before 1979, when all of Europe joined the Brits to contest the Cup. Thus Lanny is probably the greatest U.S. Ryder Cup player ever.

But he was not without flaws—namely, putting. While 1991 was one of his best years and he won in Hawaii in January, he could have won five times, maybe more. He led the Masters after twenty-six holes, and had a four-foot putt for par on the twenty-seventh. He missed it. Then he reached across the hole to backhand the remainder. Missed that, too, and had a six where he might easily have scored a four. On the other hand, Wadkins hung around admirably for the rest of the event and wound up in third place, two behind the winner, Woosnam. Lanny looked tortured as his fourth-round playing partner Olazábal surveyed shots and putts as if he were trying to memorize the contours molded in the ground. Could Wadkins avoid Langer and Olly at Kiawah? They had the slow-motion kryptonite to beat him.

From the first moment of the Couples, Wadkins, Floyd practice round at the Ocean Course, Raymond painted on his game face and never took it off. Having a brother golf professional on his bag did not mean that Floyd found out that Jim Kelechi was from suburban Cleveland or that he listened to R.E.M. or that he had been a baseballer, too, and had once struck out eighteen in a high school game. Ray didn't ask. "Fill that," he said after hitting an iron shot, pointing at his divot hole. He wanted yardages. The assistant pro made his best guess, and although he knew the four-month-old course as well as anyone, there were no laser range-finders back then, and no pin sheet on this day. Raymond let young Jim know when he thought his estimates had been wrong, but when he stuck one close, his pro/caddie got no credit. On the green, Floyd held his hand out for his cleaned golf ball, his eyes on the hole, not exchanging a glance with his employee.

His eyes. Everyone talked about his eyes. They looked a little crazy during the heat of battle, as though he'd been transported to another world. He was not someone who chatted when he had the bit in his teeth. "He had a snarly side, a need to be nasty to play well," observes veteran journalist Sirak. "At Shinnecock in '95, he yelled at me because I had a cigar in my mouth. 'Get away from me with that,' he said. The cigar wasn't lit."

Floyd's father, L. B. Floyd, was the pro at the enlisted man's course at the U.S. Army base in Fort Bragg, North Carolina. "When I grew up," Floyd told a writer, "golf was a gambling game, and that was the fascination of it for me." The Cleveland Indians offered teenaged Ray a minor league job and the University of North Carolina dangled a spot on its golf team but neither could compare to the morale, welfare, and recreation derived from playing for and winning a bet at golf. Ray was a gambler at fifteen, a pro at nineteen, and a winner on the Tour at twenty. And he was a rounder.

In that golden age for hedonists, when an amphetamine and a sugar doughnut was the breakfast of champions, Doug Sanders and Al Besselink were chairmen of the board, and Ray was their apprentice. Pretty Boy Floyd wore tight pants with no back pockets and walked like he was cracking walnuts between his butt cheeks. Oh, the stories you hear! Perhaps Ray's dalliance with the Ladybyrds tells the tale well enough. Five Jersey girls—four brunettes and a blonde, four guitars and a set of drums—were a late sixties soft rock group who performed topless. Floyd invested in the band, which moved inexorably from the East Coast to Lake Tahoe and Vegas. Despite impressive choreography and real skill with their instruments, the Ladybyrds faded away. And Ray might have, too, if not for the former Maria Fraietta, who married Ray in 1973 and told him to commit himself to golf or find another job. He committed, and won—twenty-two times on the Tour, one more than Lanny. Other players avoided eye contact with Ray at crunch time, fearing what came to be known as the Look.

Despite wins in three of the four majors, and very close calls at the British, Floyd, unlike Wadkins, did not do well in the Ryder Cup. His low point came in '83, at the PGA National, where he played four and lost four. But Ray commanded a lot of respect, and he'd won the PGA Championship, so it was no surprise when the PGA of America named him captain of its 1989 team. The surprise—a mild one, really—was Dave Stockton selecting him for the '91 squad. No one else had ever been a nonplaying Ryder Cup captain and then a player. At forty-nine, he was the oldest player Team USA had ever had. With his 7-13-3 record, he'd lost more matches than any American ever. But he could putt, and he was motivated.

Between the Cup and the majors, old campaigners like Floyd had a history with virtually every other great player in the world. The one guy who really rang his bell was Faldo. Nick owned Ray so thoroughly—and Ray was so competitive, and Nick so haughty—that friendship looked impossible. In Faldo's first-ever Ryder Cup match at Royal Lytham in '77, he and Peter Oosterhuis beat Floyd and Lou Graham. The next day the big Brits beat Ray and Jack Nicklaus. Nick beat Ray again the next time they played each other in the Ryder Cup, in foursomes in '83. And in April 1990, Faldo made it 4 and 0. When Ray coughed up a four-shot lead with six to play, Faldo and Floyd had tied for first at the Masters (her husband didn't have the Look all week, Mrs. Floyd recalled). On the first play-off hole, number ten at Augusta National, Floyd had a fifteen-foot uphill putt for birdie three and the win—but left it short. After hitting his drive on eleven, Ray ducked hurriedly into one of the few loos available to a player at Augusta National—a lovely spot in the piney woods to the left of the tee—and afterward he had to hurry to his ball in the dying light. Playing too fast, apparently, Ray yanked his second shot into the water hazard. Nick stuck his arms into a green jacket a few minutes later.

But now, two full weeks before the big event—and in a mere practice round—Raymond Loran Floyd was wearing the Look. Not a good thing for his caddie. With the round concluded, that sweet moment had arrived when the golfer opens his wallet and says, "Thanks, great job." But Ray stayed in the zone. He gestured toward the three Bridgestone golf balls in the cart. "You can have those," he said to Kelechi. And that was his pay. Golf balls for a golf pro was like paying an Eskimo snowballs for leading a seal hunt.

The assistant pro did not react for a second. During the day he'd found an old Top-Flite, a hacker's ball, and put it in the cart. "Can I have that one too?" Jim asked.

Ray glared. He was ready for the Ryder Cup.

PART TWO
THE GATHERING STORM

"David Stockton, the American team captain, and several of the players acted in a most regrettable fashion . . . as if winning was a matter of life and death."

—*Seve Ballesteros, in* Seve, *his autobiography*

"A little bit of Seve goes a long way."

—*Curtis Strange*

6

MONDAY, SEPTEMBER 23

Dave Stockton drove the thirty-three miles from Kiawah to Charleston National Airport to greet Team Europe. Bernard Gallacher was delighted with the courtesy of his host's gesture. The pleasure, however, would be short-lived, and the welcome would come to seem less an omen of amity than a symbol of power. The game started the moment the wheels touched down.

Team Europe had cleared customs in New York, stretched its long (Faldo) and short (Woosnam) legs, and arrived in Charleston in good spirits. After a bit of media hubbub in the terminal and flag-waving from European fans—including two chubby toddlers fanning tiny Union Jacks back and forth—the lads were surprised and even a bit put off by the discovery that each of them had been assigned his own black stretch limo and driver.

"Daft," said Colin Montgomerie. The players, coaches, and everyone's wives could have fit in just one of the land yachts. Were the Americans trying to deprive their guests of meaningful team time, or were they attempting to put them on their heels with a we're-richer-than-you gesture?

Still, it was exciting. Lesley Gallacher poked her husband in the ribs as they rolled down Sam Rittenberg Boulevard. "Look at all the flags, dear," she said. Seemingly every gas station, restaurant, and bar flew a flag or draped itself in red-white-blue bunting. The motorcade passed a club whose marquee shouted, "Welcome Ryder Cup. Shag! Shag! Shag!" This would have caused snickering in the English-speaking limos. In Georgialina, the shag is a dance whose complicated steps become easier the more you drink, and the louder the "beach music" booms from the classic bands of the genre, the Tams and the Drifters. But to English, Irish, Scottish, and Welsh ears, *shag* means sexual union, used as a noun or a verb. The sign would therefore have provided a juicy straight line for the humorous Feherty, but he does not remember seeing it. Pity.

The idea of shagging as a party activity reminded the visitors that it was on them to adapt to the lingo of the locals. For example, when a Yank wished to concede a putt, he'd say, "That's good." The Continental way was to say, "OK," or "Given." A player who'd qualified for the Ryder Cup in the States was said to be "on the team" while Europe had players who were "in the side." A good American player had "guts" while a brave Euro had "bottle." An ongoing match with neither team/side ahead was "even" in the Colonies; "nothing in it" described the situation from Europe's point of view. An American would be "tired" after a day of battle with the Ocean Course; the Brits and Irish in the side would be "knackered."

There was the PGA Tour on one side of the ocean and the Volvo European PGA Tour on the other. The United States hosted the Ryder Cup; Europe staged the *Johnnie Walker* Ryder Cup. (That's right, they'd sold the name of the holy of holies to a bottler of blended Scotch. Shag off if you don't like it.)

From Sam Rittenberg, the motorcade turned left onto Main Street, a much more rural thoroughfare than its name suggested. Main became Bohicket Road. (Bohicket, rhyming with thicket . . . that sounded right.) Houses along the rural way were modest, single-story dwellings, set back from the street, shadowed by palms and pines, with moss-stained shingle roofs, some of them surely occupied by descendants of the Low Country's original settlers and slaves. Moments before it pivoted sideways to let a sailboat pass, the two-ton Devilles rolled over the metal decking of a rickety old swing bridge over the Stono River, part of the Intracoastal Waterway. For a moment, the smell of salt and sea filled the air. Farther on—past the Piggly Wiggly supermarket—old oaks on either side of the road joined branches above it, creating an eight-mile-long tunnel, a sun-dappled dreamscape that reminded you of Magnolia Lane at Augusta National or the entrance to Tara, the plantation house in *Gone with the Wind.* A handful of churches stood like white sentinels in the brooding coastal forest.

•

Of all of the men in the limousines, the twenty-eight-year-old Montgomerie might have had the most reason to introspect. He'd never played in the Ryder Cup before. He didn't know what to expect or how he would do, of course, and he and Eimear were still newlyweds, together for the first time on a very big stage. But his other preoccupation was with his mum. Elizabeth "Maggie" Montgomerie had been the warm, enthusiastic counterweight to her husband, James, a by-the-book Scottish ex-army man. In 1967, James took a job in Yorkshire, managing the Fox's Biscuits (cookie) factory, whereupon Maggie and the children took up golf (thus Monty's English accent, although he is, he says, "Scottish through and through"). Douglas was six and Colin was a thin four-year-old with a soft helmet of blond curls when the family moved to England. Young Colin liked golf, but other games involving swinging a stick at a ball held equal fascination. He opened the bowling for Strathallan, his public school, and usually had to face spinners, which he hated. It was a wicket or a boundary for Colin when the bowler threw a googly.[1] In hockey, Colin and Douglas formed an effective scoring combination, although Colin had trouble keeping his swing below his knees as the rules required.

"We scored a lot of goals," Colin recalled, "and I injured a lot of goalkeepers."

Through it all, there was Maggie, an unusually with-it sportswoman. She played off a nine, and she strongly supported

1 Talking about cricket here. In baseball terms, Colin was the starting pitcher and the power hitter, but he disliked curveballs, which he tended to hit very far or miss completely. What's referred to as "public school" in most of the UK would be called private school in the U.S. The student uniform at Strathallan included a tweed sport coat and a kilt.

Leeds United football (soccer) team and her youngest son's athletics. In 1987, after college in the United States and a glittering amateur career, Colin found himself with five hundred other aspirants in Spain, attempting to qualify for the Volvo European PGA Tour. Maggie knew her son; she'd raised a perfectionist. He would appreciate a bit of perfection in his downtime during this stressful event. So Mrs. Montgomerie dashed down to La Manga and the apartment that Colin had rented for himself and his caddie, and cooked all their meals. Setting aside the pans and ladles, she joined the boys at the golf course and watched every shot her son hit.

"Lung cancer," Douglas had said on the phone that morning in April 1990. Maggie had smoked for thirty-five of her fifty-two years. Colin's life was a blur after that. In June, he married the lovely Eimear in a big, formal wedding. Mum attended, smiling for the camera in a wide-brimmed fuchsia hat, revealing to no one outside the family that she was ill. But the cancer had already metastasized. When she died a few months later, Colin lost his way. He had, he told a writer, "this tremendous sense of things left unsaid. It's very frustrating to think that I might not have adequately told her how much I appreciated everything she did for me in my life. How much I loved her."

In tournaments following his mother's death, Montgomerie stared without focus into space, his mind wandering sadly and inexorably to Maggie. Finally, he willed himself to snap out of it. Dedicating a win or a goal to a departed loved one is a corny convention in the world of the perspiring arts, but sometimes it works. Maggie had always loved watching the Ryder Cup on

TV; in early '91, Monty vowed to make the Ryder Cup side in her memory.[2] When he won the Scandinavian Masters at Drottningholm, Sweden, in August—Seve was second, Woosnam third—he'd accomplished his goal. The three stood on a podium together, like medal winners at the Olympics. Only Seve finished the year of qualifying with more Ryder Cup points.

The cars emerged from the shadows. South Carolina Governor Carroll Campbell and Ninth District highway commissioner Robert Harrell had led the effort to get Bohicket widened over the few miles nearest the entrance to Kiawah, turning it into a dual carriageway—or as Americans called it, a four-lane highway. Left turn onto the island, into the resort. *Kiawah Island* in flowing cursive on a low wooden sign: modest, understated, classy.

The limos rolled slowly on the serpentine entrance road, with wild jungle growth and the vast coastal wetland on either side. The sea-scented air sharpened the appetite and promised breaking waves nearby. Right turn just past the second green at Marsh Point Golf Club—a short hole (par three in the local parlance)—and then alongside the eighteenth fairway to the graceful, dark brown Kiawah Island Inn. No one got out his Amex or Diners card; each party was guided directly and decorously to its two- or three-bedroom condo in Building 500—

2 For Team USA, qualifying for the Ryder Cup was spread out over two years; but Europe chose its team based on the twenty-six-week performance in the year in which the event was held.

not part of the Inn—and known to the staff as "the high rise." Building 500 had five stories, and stunning ocean views. It was late afternoon now, too late to hit a golf ball or to tour the Ocean Course, a nine-mile, fifteen-minute drive away. The team settled in, changed shirts and shoes, and unpacked.[3] A few strolled down to the wide beach to admire the Atlantic close up. Shrimp boats bobbed in the middle distance.

At sunset, players and coaches[4] convened for an oyster roast at Mingo Point, a lovely piece of high ground in the marsh near the entrance to the resort. Torrance, Feherty, and especially Woosnam quaffed amber nectar served in the strange American style—ice cold. At the other end of the drinking scale sat Langer. He'd been in eastbound jets most of the previous twenty-four hours; Seve needn't have worried about the punctuality or the preparedness of the pious, hard-working German, physically the fittest man in the side. And like his hero, Gary Player, Langer was as much professional traveler as professional golfer. After his ninth-place finish in the ANA

3 There was a lot to put in the closet. For off the course: two blazers, two pairs of slacks, a suit, two pairs of dress shoes, four shirts, and two ties, all provided by Hugo Boss and Oscar Jacobson; on-course wear from Glenmuir consisted of twelve pairs of slacks, twelve sports shirts, two sweaters, a rainsuit, two pairs of golf shoes, and many pairs of socks. The U.S. team had a similar mammoth wardrobe for the six days of the Ryder Cup, except that it also had a bit of camo.

4 As his assistant coach, Gallacher had retained the diplomatic and polite Manuel Piñero, a native of Madrid who had played in two Ryder Cups, in 1981 and 1985. Piñero had succeeded spectacularly in Europe's breakthrough in '85, winning four out of five points, including a defeat of Wadkins in singles.

Sapporo Open, his flights from Tokyo had connected so perfectly that he had arrived at Kiawah a few hours ahead of his teammates. He'd looked up from his work on the Ocean Course practice tee when Concorde did its flyby that afternoon, answered a reporter's questions—as always, Herr Langer was crisp and correct but not particularly quotable—before heading to the putting green. And there the straightest of straight arrows practiced a stroke so avant garde it had no precedent, and no imitators.

•

Langer's whack-a-doodle technique had been incubated in 1988—his year in golf hell, the most depressing time of his life. He thought often about quitting. All his problems and all his pain were concentrated in one little club, the golfer's scalpel, the bane of his existence: the putter. Once, he four-putted from three feet. Several times he double-hit short putts—each tap of ball on putter counts as a stroke, of course. Match play opponents wouldn't concede any putt longer than the length of a scorecard, so ham-handed was Bernhard from in close.

He began to sense a new element in his gallery: people there not to observe his brilliant ball striking, but instead gathered to witness his tragicomic twitches, like race car fans hoping for a crash. That one of the world's greatest athletes could not perform the simplest act in his sport seems mind-boggling, but sometimes self-consciousness trumps instinct even in elite performers. Basketball stars with the most amazing hand-eye coordination have lost the ability to make free throws. Baseball players—most famously, Chuck Knoblauch and Steve Sax—were horrified to discover that they couldn't make the shortest throw in the game, from second base to first. Another major leaguer, Mackey Sasser, a catcher, suddenly couldn't reliably toss the ball back to the pitcher. Among all sports, short circuiting is probably most common in golf; like others before him and since, Bernhard was trapped in the cruel embrace of the yips, as if his digits were stuck in a Chinese finger trap. The more he pulled against his ineffable foe, the tighter its grip.

How did it feel? Langer answered the question straightforwardly in his straightforwardly titled autobiography: *Bernhard Langer: My Autobiography*. "It is an involuntary and uncontrollable movement of the muscles. . . . It is a churning of the stomach, an extreme nervousness. It is a loss of nerve."

What could he do? "I asked the Lord, 'Why me? What have I done to deserve this?' " When God gave no specific answer, Langer did what he had always done: He went back to the practice ground and worked his ass off.

On a putting green in Frankfurt a few days before the start of the '89 German Open, Langer labored with five clubs to no effect. Maybe it wasn't a hardware problem. He'd experimented with his grip before, of course, in scores of ways and hundreds of times. But in the second or third hour of the session he tried anchoring the putter against the inside of his left arm, and then gripping club and left arm and all with his right hand. The split cross-handed forearm grip had revealed itself. The angels sang. *Gott im Himmel*—it worked! "I made three- and four-footers, right away," Langer recalls. "I just had to rock my shoulders." When he won the Spanish Open that summer—his first win in more than a year—Langer used his wacky arrangement of hands and arms to shoot 67 in the final round, with only twenty-seven putts.

The other early arrivers to Kiawah from Team Europe were Sam Torrance and Paul Broadhurst. Paul had done quite well in the B.C. Open in upstate New York, finishing ninth, on 66-69-71-71, seven under par, good for $20,800 (U.S. Ryder Cupper Steve "The Volcano" Pate shot 68-70-68-70, one shot and $5,000 better than the Englishman; Wayne Levi, the weakest link in the American chain, shot 74-72 and missed the cut). Sam and Paul played a practice round at the Ocean and had lots to say about it at the oyster roast. Gallacher took the floor to review the schedule and to remark on the course generally and on one hole particularly: the par three, extraordinarily scary seventeenth. Its green was relatively large but was canted the wrong way. You couldn't be short or right because of a lagoon, or left because of meteor craters and sand dotted with random plantings of sea oats. "There's simply no let-out around the green," the captain said.

"What's the pressure of this thing really like?" Feherty asked his best friend, Torrance, for the umpteenth time. They called each other idiot, fairy, Jessie, or arsehole. Hard to know which endearment David chose this time.

"It's like having a kid," answered Sam; in other words, an almost indescribable thrill and responsibility.

Except for the mosquitoes, Gallacher found the evening delightful. He felt a sense of relief. No one in the United States knew what a struggle getting to this point had been, with the infighting between the British PGA and the Volvo European PGA Tour so brutal that more than once Bernard had offered to resign. The dispute revolved around money and power: What would be the split of the juicy proceeds, who would select future Ryder Cup venues, and who got to name the captain. Things had been simpler when the Ryder Cup cost rather than made money. Golf pros in the United States then belonged to the PGA of America and the pros in Great Britain pledged allegiance to the British PGA. But tournament golf grew big and rich on both sides of the pond, and the touring pros in the United States sensibly declared their independence in 1968, becoming, eventually, the PGA Tour.[5]

It was the same basic deal in Europe a few years later. But there was a problem: the BPGA—the club professional organization—believed it should have the greatest say in how the Cup was administered. The golfers who actually put on the show disagreed; veiled threats to "not support" the Cup floated back and forth between the two camps.

Adding to Gallacher's unease was the fact that he was both a club pro and a touring pro. He traveled to play in tournaments, but his main source of income came from his labor at Wentworth Club near London, where he'd been the head pro for years.

This complicated and colossally boring bureaucratic dispute—

5 "After giving up the tournaments, they didn't want to lose the Ryder Cup too," recalls Bob Goalby, one of the architects of the Tournament Players Division of the PGA of America.

which was not much covered in the U.S. press—weighed heavily on Captain Gallacher. He had been a stalwart member of eight teams, and had assisted Captain Jacklin in three more. As a player, he'd beaten Trevino, Nicklaus, and Wadkins in singles. The Ryder Cup was in his blood. So he soldiered on, and took two trips to Kiawah to prepare for the big event.

On the second of these, a few months before the event, he had played the Ocean with architect Dye and with U.S. captain Stockton. Bernard and Dave had a little Ryder Cup history already: In a singles match in St. Louis in 1971, the Californian holed a fifteen-footer on the final hole to salvage a tie. Gallacher found Stockton's "I-just won-the-Open!" reaction distasteful, but he liked him.

"He is a really nice fellow," Bernard wrote in his book *Captain at Kiawah*, "but underneath there has always been a tough competitor, and I was left in no two minds on my trip to Kiawah that he was desperate to lead his Cup team to victory. I mean desperate!"

The mellow Monday evening ended. Captain Gallacher had a hands-off coaching style, but—worried that the standoffish Faldo might go off by himself after the morning press conference, and how would *that* look—he assigned pairings and starting times for the first practice round. He reminded his squad that breakfast and all other informal meals would be taken in his and Lesley's spacious three-bedroom condo. "All right, chaps, see you at half seven. Sleep well." Off went the group into the gentle night.

Kiawah Island can take your breath away, but other islands on the ragged southern South Carolina coast have the same oak trees draped in Spanish moss, identical dunes, the same gators, and similar sinister beauty. On one of them, Parris Island, forty miles south as the egret flies, the soundtrack is the rhythmic impact of the black boots of jogging jarheads, and the occasional thin whine of a mosquito near your ear. After a few days or weeks, the first person disappears from the speech of the newcomers to the island. There is no *I* in *team:* "This recruit has enjoyed marksmanship training. . . . This recruit will serve wherever he is needed."

When those recruits had to stand at attention or remain motionless on patrol, they were not allowed to shoo away the sand fleas or skeeters bedeviling their noses or necks. They gotta eat, too, the drill instructors said. Besides, the sound of a slap could give away your position to the enemy, endangering your life, which is bad, and the lives of others, which is far worse.

The final act in the warrior training at the Marine Corps Recruit Depot on Parris Island is called the Crucible, a hellish fifty-four hours of combat endurance and problem solving involving forty-eight miles of running and obstacle-coursing while sleeping and eating very little and while carrying full gear and a rifle. The USMC website description of one of the Day Two activities was surely written by a Marine: "Remove simulated casualties from a simulated danger area consisting of artillery simulators." Day Three begins with reveille at three A.M., and a fast nine-mile hike back to base. Then the elite band of survivors stands as still as statues for the Eagle Globe and Anchor ceremony, marking its transition from recruits to Marines. Then it's all-you-can-eat steak and eggs, and a nap.

But it wasn't just proximity to Parris Island that gave the '91 Ryder Cup its martial overtone. Nor was it because Charleston contained The Citadel, the Military College of South Carolina; a navy base; an air force base; and lots of retired military. No, pride in the armed forces was a national phenomenon in '91.

The big deal had occurred in January, when the elder President Bush led the UN coalition that expelled Iraqi invaders from Kuwait and blasted them almost to Baghdad during their retreat. After six weeks of precision bombs and Schwarzkopf, the coalition had won a resounding victory. Then came another triumph, this one more important but less splashy than the successful prosecution of the Gulf War.

Tom Brokaw led off the *NBC Nightly News* on August 21 with "Good evening. This is a day for bold print in history"—because an attempted coup by hardliners in the USSR had failed. The Union of Soviet Socialist Republics and its Communist Party circled the drain. The Cold War had been won.

In September, Bush formally recognized Estonia, Latvia, and Lithuania, fragments from the crumbling Union of Soviet Socialist Republics. Then GHWB grounded the U.S. fleet of nuclear-bomb-armed B-52s that had been patrolling the air since 1955, and removed the arsenal of ground-launched, nuclear-tipped Titan missiles from alert status.

"Since the Persian Gulf War, there's been a new kind of pride in the country, and that's come into golf," said Chip Beck, a month before the Ryder Cup at Kiawah. "It's like, 'Hey, wait a minute. You can't kick us forever. We're going to jump up and bite you.' We've got some things to prove."

The United States, the putative conqueror of two Evil Empires in one year, stood tall in the afterglow. Patriotism filled the air in Charleston that sunny weekend in September as palpably as love or gnats. The two golf nuts at the top of the government amplified the vibe. Vice President Dan Quayle would grace Kiawah in person on Sunday while President Bush would watch on TV from nearby Sea Island, Georgia (and deliver a televised pep talk to Team USA). In short, this mere game of golf had assumed a national importance and an emotional us-against-them feeling without precedent in the United States except, perhaps, during the Cold War–era Olympics.

Team Europe didn't like it.

"When Pavin and Pate emerged in Desert Storm hats, that was the end," Montgomerie would recall. "Were they completely oblivious to the fact that we had troops over in the Gulf too?"

"This was one of the worst Ryder Cups, in terms of attitude between players and the hostility of the U.S. crowd," Langer wrote in *My Autobiography*. "It is not a war; it is a game. I felt it got out of hand and the spectators got very rowdy. It was all over the top."

Apprised of Langer's and Monty's comments, Peter Jacobsen digs the knuckles of his index fingers into the corners of his eyes. "Boo-hoo," he says.

7

TUESDAY, SEPTEMBER 24

Midmorning: The white polyethylene top of the enormous media tent undulated in a light breeze. Within its twelve thousand square feet were most of the seven hundred journalists accredited for the event. Twelve thousand! Seven hundred! No one could remember a group of golf typists so large or a top so big.

The irresistible source for an old-guy perspective sat like a king in a space reserved for *Golfweek* magazine. Bob Drum, ex of *The Pittsburgh Press,* belonged to an era in which the beat writer for a star's hometown paper became the local hero's de facto spokesman. Dan Jenkins and Ben Hogan of Fort Worth; Kaye Kessler and Jack Nicklaus of Columbus, Ohio; and Drum and Arnold Palmer of western Pennsylvania. "We were headquartered in a loft at Pinehurst in '51," said Drum, a bluff Irishman whose voice and exterior favored *60 Minutes* mainstay Andy Rooney, except that "The Drummer" usually had a drink and an f-bomb ready for launch.[1]

1 Like Rooney, Drum also did short segments within larger programs on CBS Television. "The Drummer's Beat" was featured during golf telecasts.

"It seemed like there were more British writers than spectators. There couldn't have been more than a half-dozen American writers." Now, there were two hundred journalists from around the United States, plus another fifty or so technicians and on-air "talent" from USA Network and NBC.

"This is the most extensively covered sporting event over three days in history," said Andy O'Brien, the manager of media relations for the PGA of America. "Almost two billion people around the world will have the opportunity to watch this year's Ryder Cup."

As the brides entered the church the room fell silent, more or less. Into the vast marquee walked Captain Gallacher; his assistant, the short, suave Piñero; and the twelve stalwarts of Team Europe. Blazered plenipotentiaries followed in their wake. This would be the media's only chance to talk to the competitors all week, a situation very much desired by the players. The extremely limited journalistic access at the Masters and the Memorial is one reason those events are held so dear by their participants, for despite the opportunity for credible free publicity—which can raise a Q rating and thus endorsement income—most big-time golf pros place writers on a level with life insurance salesmen, or worse. To the pros the dispensers of golf prose are time wasters, stupidly asking the same questions over and over while staying alert as little birds for a slipup.

Langer is eloquent on the subject: "Especially in Europe, they make up stuff. They tell lies or things not proven. They have hidden agendas, some very bad. A writer in London was told to dig up dirt on Faldo, or resign, which he did. . . . And in a Ryder Cup year, they write about Ryder Cup every single day, not once a week, like here [in the United States]."

The press conference commenced but not in the orderly way Gallacher had expected, with the players and coaches seated at a raised table, and one question at a time. The PGA of America had instead decided on a locker-room-style proceeding. So Bernard and his team spread out in the tent and ladies and gentlemen with notepads, microphones, and tape recorders clotted around them.

Someone asked Feherty if the Ocean Course looked like the links courses back home. "It's not like something in Ireland or Scotland, it's like something from Mars," he said. "Like a lot of modern courses, victory won't always go to the guy who hits the ball the best, but the one who takes all the rubbish."

"I don't like walking around it," said Woosnam, a reference to the soft, sandy footing.

Faldo told his group that the Ryder Cup was a great sporting event, not just a great golf match, and it could do without all the red-white-and-blue hype surrounding it this week.

Seve seconded Nick, noting that Nicklaus had recently referred to this year's competition as a war. "It's not a war," said Seve. "It's golf."

The voluble Feherty opined that the Ryder Cup is a celebration of the game, or should be, and that no acrimony existed between the European players and the American team. That was mostly true. While Azinger had no love connection with Faldo or Seve, the top European golfers competed ten times or so in the States every year, providing enough contact for friendliness, if not friendships. Langer's principal residence was in

Florida, and he'd married a girl from Louisiana. And Woosnam, who considered the Ryder Cup a biennial party, was in the midst of conducting a sort of lager diplomacy with his supposed enemy ("I couldn't believe how much he was partying that week!" Beck recalled).

The group around the captain heard him express surprise at the buzz in the room, and at the number of buzzers. "It's always been a very, very important match to me and the Europeans and the British," he said. "It amazes me that it has just suddenly caught on here."

Gallacher answered more questions while looking around the vast interior space, the sunny day illuminating the tent's ceiling and sides. The biggest contingent of journalists huddled around Seve, while slightly smaller groups groped for interesting quotes from Woosie, Nick, Torrance, and Langer. But no one with a pen was talking to his lesser lights; Gilford and Broadhurst looked as if they were waiting for a bus. This wouldn't do at all. The obvious slights to the rookies could be bad for morale. Seething at what he called chaos, Gallacher summoned his team up onto the platform. Then the microphone didn't work.

"What a shambles," Gallacher would write. "The American officials had known for six months when I would be bringing in my team but had made a complete hash of it. What a start!"

While the captain of Team Europe felt the first stirrings of anger at how his hosts were getting things wrong, he might have been comforted to think how many things they were getting right. The thousands of successfully handled infrastructure and logistical details might be symbolized by the raw, sawn ends of the oak limbs on Bohicket Road. With scant parking on the island, nearly everyone would be bussed in from Charleston or from the lots near the resort entrance, the PGA of America having retained "every bus in South Carolina," according to its president, Jim O'Brien. The PGA of America's bus bill: about five hundred thousand dollars. Someone had had the foresight to compare the dimensions of a popular model, the MCI 102A3 motor coach—it was eleven feet high and almost nine feet wide—with the space available in that tunnel of oaks surrounding the road to Kiawah. Thus the trim job.

The two hundred buses were assigned drivers and routes; spots to load, unload, and park; and places to refuel. Roads were closed, traffic was rerouted, and water traffic was restricted; the Stono River, John F. Limehouse, and Wappoo Creek bridges were closed during peak hours. No one wanted an amphibious landing of gate-crashers on the beach adjacent to the venue. School was canceled on Friday, and an anti-price-gouging ordinance was passed and enforced. A couple of giant gators were removed from Ocean Course lagoons and relocated God knows where. Armies of food-service people readied Sternos, roast turkey, Chardonnay, and oceans of soft drinks and beer. Chick-fil-A vended sandwiches; Pizza Hut sold its pies.

Clothing and golf gear companies shipped tons of logoed merchandise; golf pros Jim Kelechi and Dale Mercer prepared to sell it. Logoed shirts, of course, and framed posters for $530; sunscreen for $13; beach towels for $35; and caps sold for $17.

Tents and trailers dotted the golf course perimeter, sheltering tournament administration, retail, and corporate hospitality—the best of the latter belonging to Kiawah Resort Associates. Since the smallish clubhouse was not quite finished—and would have been inadequate for the job anyway—two extra-large, air-conditioned trailers had been imported to serve as dressing rooms and informal headquarters for the players. They sat down below the clubhouse, uncomfortably close to each other; when the ebullient Deborah Couples was in the area, everyone on both teams knew it.

NBC TV producer Larry Cirillo organized his little army, most of which was being housed in Charleston. "They have to leave the hotel at three-thirty A.M. to get on the island by four-thirty in time to be on the air by eight," Cirillo told *The Post and Courier*. "We've got lunch coming in at five-thirty in the morning. Even the production and announcing teams have to be up by five A.M. in order to get on the site for rehearsal at six-thirty."

Against all odds and a moving mountain of blowing sand, Superintendent George Frye and his crew had grown the Ocean Course grass to wall-to-wall perfection. Dunes—soon to be modified by thousands of spectators' feet—were molded into natural shapes. Rules officials, tournament administrators, gallery marshals, and other volunteers prepared for the golf event of the century.

Market forces and entrepreneurial spirit took care of what Kiawah Island Resort, the Charleston Chamber of Commerce, NBC, and the PGA of America did not. Delta Airlines added flights. Golf courses and hotels up the coast arranged package deals that included Ryder Cup tickets. The influx of visitors would have to be entertained when they were not watching Seve and Freddie; young Mike Borders came down from the Grand Strand—aka Myrtle Beach—to help. By summoning talent from all over this great country, Borders was able to retain fifty ecdysiasts to wiggle in spotlights on tables and a stage every night from Thursday through Sunday at the King Street Palace.[2] Tournament manager Kathy Boles stated for the record that the PGA of America had nothing to do with the performance, and had refused an ad for it in the official tournament program. But Boobapalooza got a nice publicity boost from Charleston's major newspaper, *The Post and Courier.* The headline to the story on Page 13-A of the Thursday paper read, "Ryder spectators offered another eyeful." Embedded in the short piece was a head-and-shoulders shot of Tiffany Hills—a lovely gal with big brunette hair and big brown eyes—the star and spokesperson of the Crazy Horse Revue. Much more of her dermis had appeared in other publications, she said, such as *Thigh High, Hustler's Busty Beauties,* and *Swank.*

She didn't mind being called a stripper, Ms. Hills told reporter Karen Avenoso: " 'Exotic dancer' or 'featured entertainer' or 'stripper,' to me, it's all the same." She got started in the business, she said, when her boss in an office kept suggesting things, "so I decided to take a job where I would be sexually harassed and make enough money to deal with it. Now, I'm self-employed."

2 The King Street Palace was more an auditorium than a nightclub. Post-Hugo, Oprah Winfrey had broadcast from there.

Since 1977, Charleston had hosted an annual international nerd-fest called the Spoleto Festival—chamber music, art, theater, jazz, symphony—but that was as a church supper compared to the '91 Ryder Cup. Someone from the vigilant Chamber of Commerce anticipated a conflict between the armada of giant buses and the eleven little churches on Bohicket Road. Greater St. John African Methodist Episcopal, Calvary AME, Bethlehem United Methodist, Johns Island Presbyterian, and the rest were, of course, in the habit of conducting services on Sunday mornings. Problem: The PGA of America would be conducting Ryder Cup singles matches on Sunday, beginning at nine A.M. Would you take care of this, Gary?

Gary Schaal, a golf pro from Myrtle Beach via Akron, Ohio, had the interpersonal skills of a diplomat or—same thing—a very good golf professional. As the PGA of America's national secretary in 1988 (he would ascend to vice president in 1990 and president in '92), he had been in on the discussion when the idea was floated to reroute the Ryder Cup from PGA West to the Ocean Course. He was against it. "I said, 'Guys, wait a minute,'" Schall recalls. "'There's no road, no clubhouse, and no notoriety [for the still unbuilt Ocean]. And the backup course at Kiawah, Turtle Point—the pros will shoot fifty-seven or fifty-eight on that.' But the South Carolina governor four-laned the road, the bus companies and the Chamber of Commerce were incredible, and Dye and the PGA did a magical job."

Schaal's first Ryder Cup had been the 1987 edition at Muirfield Village. "The most magnificent event I'd ever been to," he recalls. "If you didn't tear up at that opening ceremony, you didn't have a heart. I saw world-class athletes getting autographs from each other while everyone's dinner got cold. . . . I had mixed feelings about our loss that year. I didn't think it was all bad for the Ryder Cup.

"Were the crowds very boisterous at the Belfry in '89? I'd describe them otherwise. Especially when you compare them to European football [soccer], the behavior was very good, up until late in the day when quite a few lagers had been poured. But when a line had been crossed, Ballesteros or the captain would calm the crowd."

Schaal resolved the Bohicket Road churches versus Ryder Cup singles problem very directly. He knocked on the white front door of one of the churches—was it Reverend Brown at Greater St. John African Methodist Episcopal?—Schaal can't remember. As he introduced himself and his mission to the minister, the holy man frowned. "You're asking me and my fellow pastors not to do what we've been doing for many, many years," the man said, and his visitor felt a sinking feeling. Then the reverend laughed—gotcha!—and told the relieved Schaal that rescheduling would be no problem. He'd call his two brothers and a cousin—all of whom led flocks on Bohicket Road—to get the word out. All agreed to open their doors on Sunday, September 29, in the afternoon, rather than in the morning, when thousands of partisans would be praying for the demigods inside the yellow ropes at Kiawah Island.

Montgomerie made it through his first Ryder Cup press conference unscathed, then walked slightly uphill over eighty yards of sand and grass to the makeshift dressing room. He picked up his shoes—a new pair of Stylo Matchmakers. He slipped them on. They felt a little tight; perhaps his tootsies had swelled from his hours aboard Concorde.

Consumers opening a box from the same manufacturer found an advertising card within, with a picture of and a message from the greatest golfer in the world: "When Stylo asked me to help them develop a new generation of golf shoes, I was happy to accept. The result in the Faldo range [combines] my on-course experience with Stylo's unrivaled expertise in shoe manufacturing, gained over the past twenty years. The shoes are stylish, beautifully designed, AND made in Northampton on special lasts using advanced materials technology."

Back to Monty: "I was working away quite happily [on the practice tee] and my concern about the footwear had almost totally subsided when suddenly I noticed Nick Faldo, a veteran of seven Ryder Cups and very much the kingpin, striding toward me." The shoe endorser held a pair of the shoes he endorsed, for which Stylo paid him a hundred thousand pounds per year. "Monty," said Nick, "what size shoes do you take?" The rookie, trying very hard to do the right thing, had done the wrong thing, by slipping on Faldo's Faldo model golf boots. Mortified and apologizing profusely, Montgomerie removed one pair of Stylos and put on the other. Nick went off to begin drilling under the watchful eye of David Leadbetter.

As writer Herbert Warren Wind once said of Ben Hogan,

"He was a very *odd* man." So, too, was Nick, and in some of the same ways. In fact, Faldo held the ascetic American champion of the forties and fifties in such high regard that he practiced like him (constantly); tried, to a degree, to swing like him; and interacted with the world like him (often not well). Even those Faldo model Stylos saluted Hogan: They had thirteen spikes, not the standard twelve. Hogan had invented the concept. He thought the extra nail under the ball of the foot anchored him in the ground a little better.

Nick grew up in a plain-Jane, two-up, two-down council house (public housing, to Americans[3]) but both parents worked, and he was a doted-on only child. When at age thirteen he decided golf would be his game—after watching the 1971 Masters on the telly—Mum and Dad devoted resources to him, as did Hertfordshire. "Nick was just like us back then, a nice player, nothing special," recalls Nigel Notley, a teammate on the county youth team. "But then his game just skyrocketed." A hard worker with talent, and a pro at age nineteen, Faldo was the youngest-ever Ryder Cup player a year later—and he won all three of his matches in '77, defeating, amazingly, Floyd, Nicklaus, and Watson in the process. And in 1990, Faldo achieved an incredible honor: Player of the Year on both the U.S. and European Tours.

Not ascending, however, were his interpersonal skills, for

3 Living in a council house did not hold the same stigma as living in a housing project in the United States. England's private residences had been decimated by German bombs in World War II, so low-rent, government-backed housing had been a necessity.

Nick had a self-absorption rare even for golf. As he won on increasingly bigger stages, and had an increasing need to say something graceful, Faldo remained a bright but socially awkward teenager. He said the wrong thing or he said nothing; he did not show up for a banquet held in his honor; he forgot for all time to give credit to his first coach; and he pissed off Azinger with his condescension at the '88 Open at Muirfield.

"I don't know Nick Faldo," Sandy Lyle told John Huggan of *Golf Digest* in 1992, despite having been Nick's peer and contemporary for decades, with the same agent (IMG), and a teammate in five Ryder Cups. "I've never known Nick Faldo. If he walked past me right now he wouldn't stop to talk. He wouldn't even say hello." As Huggan would write for Sport.Scotsman.com in 2008, "the other players almost unanimously loathed him."

Faldo's relationship with the blood-curdling British media was just as bad, in part because he was so different from the previous hero of English golf, the engaging Tony Jacklin. Fleet Street referred to him as "Fold-o," as mentioned, a rude salute to the times he did not win when he could have. Another nickname was Bungalow Bill. This was not related to the Beatles song of the same name, but was a commentary—an unfair one—on his intellect. Bungalows in England have only one story. Thus, the joke was that Nick had no rooms upstairs. When the author of a Hogan biography gave him a copy on the practice tee at the U.S. Open at Southern Hills in Tulsa, Nick took the book as if he'd suddenly been presented with a plate of moo goo gai pan or a bust of Balzac. He walked away, too gobsmacked to say a word. "He thanks you *very* much," said his caddie, Fanny Sunesson, giving the impression that she'd become an expert at picking up the pieces for her boss.

Although he was off his peak, having won only one event all year, the Carroll's Irish Open at Killarney—thereby falling to third in the world ranking behind Woosnam and Olazábal—1991 was still the prime of Mr. Nick Faldo. Within a year of the melodrama at Kiawah, he would hang out a shingle as a golf course architect; he'd begin to take helicopter pilot lessons; and he would again win the Open Championship, his fifth major. A telling moment occurred after Nick holed the winning putt at Muirfield: He handed playing partner Steve Pate his scorecard—totally blank. Faldo had been too wrapped up in his own game to keep track of anything or anyone else; Pate told Nick to put him down for a 65 (he'd shot 73).

Furthermore, the handsome, admirable, unlikable man was well on his way to becoming the greatest of all Ryder Cup players; in terms of appearances made and points won, he would exceed even Lanny. He had the composure to win a match, that was certain. In the second biggest mano a mano tournament in professional golf, the World Match Play, Faldo would win twice and finish second three times. Not that anyone got too emotional about the WMP, which was a candle compared to the forest fire of the Ryder Cup, but an incident in the 1983 event continued to burn.

In a first-round contest with Australian pro Graham Marsh, Nick hit a hot shot over the green and through the gallery on the par-four sixteenth at the West Course at Wentworth Club in suburban London. About ten seconds after it hit the green, the ball came unexpectedly back onto the surface, to within ten feet from the hole, courtesy of an impressively accurate throw or kick from a misguided spectator.

When the match referee came up to the green with Faldo and Marsh, a gallery marshal told him what had occurred. But others on the scene offered conflicting claims regarding the throw/kick/miracle bounce. The minutes dragged. The air grew tense. The ref thumbed his book *Decisions on the Rules of Golf.* Hmmm . . . Rule 19, Ball in Motion Deflected or Stopped. Hmmm . . . there, 19-1/4.1, Ball Deliberately Deflected or Stopped Through the Green by Spectator: "If there is no question that the ball would have come to rest somewhere else if X had not deflected it, the Committee must make a judgment as to where the ball would have come to rest." Deciding, apparently, that there *was* doubt about what had happened, Nick was told to play his ball where it lay. "Are you OK with this?" Faldo asked his opponent, and his opponent said he was.

Nick two-putted. Graham left his birdie try a yard short: This was the moment when Nick might have played the sportsman and conceded the putt, for who would want to win a hole under such circumstances? But Faldo let Marsh putt it, and Marsh missed. The unease in the gallery was expressed by a man—in some accounts, it was the overruled marshal—who put his hand on Nick's neck as he walked to the seventeenth tee and called him a cheating bastard.

He wasn't, of course. An official had ruled, and Nick had abided. But fans are in the field of play in golf, and when they ignore the gentleman's agreement that they should never attempt to affect the outcome, all hell breaks loose. Legality and fairness could not collide similarly at the Ryder Cup at Kiawah, could they? Would Rule Nineteen dash one slash four dot one be on everyone's lips? Nah. Too many people—witnesses!—and with the advent of radio-frequency handhelds, USA Network and NBC would have cameras peering at every shot in every match. Professional golf watchers, too, such as Tommy Horton, who described what he saw for BBC Radio. NBC TV employed foot soldier/commentators Mark McCumber, Mark Rolfing, Peter Jacobsen, and Bob Trumpy, and, in the booth, Charlie Jones and Johnny Miller. None of them were shy. On the other hand, the same dunes that often hid the players from the gallery also hid the gallery, and perhaps conferred a feeling of anonymity. Gallacher expected trouble with Rules, rulings, and irrationally exuberant fans. He discussed it with his team in his suite in Building 500.

After their warm-up, Faldo, Monty, Langer, and Richardson went out in the first group in the late morning to play their first-ever game on the frightening Ocean Course. Seven of the other eight followed; Mark James stayed behind to rest and practice. The U.S. team, its practice round completed, trooped into the media tent at two-thirty P.M. Gallacher noted with bitter amusement that the free-for-all interview format had been abandoned. Stockton told the multitude that he'd launch Lanny in the first match on Friday. With no one in front of him, the fastest player in the game might be able to play at a pace he liked. This turned out to be a canard, or a gambit, or perhaps the captain merely changed his mind. Wadkins would wind up in the third match on Friday, stuck behind slow-moving trucks named Langer and Olazábal.

What are your favorite holes? someone asked. "Seventeen,"

replied Steve Pate. "You stand on the tee and you can't see half the green. . . . It's long and intimidating." Irwin, O'Meara, and Stewart agreed. "There's no margin for error," Payne said. "You have to stand up there and hit a good golf shot." Calcavecchia chose the par-five seventh because it was reachable in two shots. "I like 'em all," said Lanny, a diplomatic response, because when he'd played the course for the first time back in April, he let it slip that he hadn't liked any of 'em.

Near the end of the day, the teams gathered for a beer and a chat about local rules. Announcement One: The bunkers would not be treated as bunkers—that is, they were not hazards. You could ground your club, hit the sand with a practice swing, or lie down and look at the sky if you wanted to. There was just so much sand and the borders were so ill-defined and natural that there was no other way to do it. (The phrase *waste area* became attached to the nongrass areas of the course, a description the Rules boys found odious. The TV announcers only made it worse by calling the sand "transitional waste area.")

Announcement Two: In foursomes—aka alternate shot—there would be no ball switching. For example, if Chip Beck was to be the driver on odd-numbered holes, he would have to announce on the first tee his make and model of ball, and he and his teammate would have to play it exclusively on every odd-numbered hole. If his teammate—say, Paul Azinger—used a ball from a different manufacturer or with a different compression (the tightness of the rubber bands stretched around the ball's core), that ball would have to be used on all the even-numbered holes. Chip couldn't use Paul's ball, and vice versa.

That night the teams attended the President's Dinner. Before attacking its tossed salads, and giving each other gifts—pewter cigarette boxes for the Euros, carriage clocks for the Yanks; Waterford crystal from Bernard to Dave, a similarly lovely piece of glass from Dave to Bernard—PGA of America CEO Jim Awtrey asked the group to bow their heads. Awtrey implored the Lord for safety, friendship, good weather, a fair competition—and a U.S. victory. Amen.

The European team sat in stunned silence.

8

WEDNESDAY, SEPTEMBER 25

5:00 A.M.

Michael D. Forcier selected an interesting way to make a living. Announcing and ad-libbing on the radio took the son of Apple Valley, Minnesota, to various rural or lightly urban outposts such as Lemmon, South Dakota; Fort Collins, Colorado; and Green Bay, Wisconsin. Eventually he made his way to St. George, South Carolina, a distant, tiny suburb of Charleston, and the home of the World Grits Festival. When he landed a gig with 95.1 WSSX-FM in North Charleston, he'd hit the big time, relatively speaking.

As Michael D, the station's morning drive-time disc jockey, Forcier adopted an irreverent on-air personality, which fit pretty well with the nose-thumbing new popular rock music called grunge. Between playing Top 40 hits by such as Nirvana, Pearl Jam, and R.E.M., Michael D employed his stock-in-trade: He woke people up. His audience, already in its truck or car on the way to work, laughed at the disoriented replies of whatever celebrity or congressman the funny Minnesotan rung up. So when this new thing came to town—the Ryder Cup—and caused the Low Country to boil with excitement, a few very early morning calls to Team Europe seemed in order.

He called this bit of shtick "Wake up the Enemy." "Good morning, Nick! Michael D here with 95SX wishing you the best of luck in the Ryder . . ." Faldo hung up, Woosnam said hi and bye, but rookie Broadhurst, who didn't know any better, engaged in a minute or two of on-air conversation. May the best team win—sorry it's not yours, said Michael D. Gallacher hadn't been sleeping well that second night on the island anyway, and the repeated calls and quick hang-ups he received (not from the DJ) didn't help. At breakfast, Bernard advised the lads to keep their phones off the hook henceforth, while he would keep his connected, in case someone really needed him. He told Stockton and the PGA of America about Charleston's crank caller and newspapers on both sides of the Atlantic ran with the story. BBC Radio retaliated by calling Forcier at four A.M. at his home the next day.

Both captains ducked into the big top to address the media. They knew they'd lost control of their message. The Seven Hundred were by now routinely using the somewhat clever "War by the Shore"—an improvement, at least, over other lame efforts at an informal title for the '91 Ryder Cup, such as "World War Tee," or, Spain's version, "The Battle of the Coast."

Portrayals of tension between the two captains were equally rampant. The dry Gallacher complained that his attempts to be jocular—how much Stockton had celebrated when he holed the putt to tie him in their Cup match in '71, and their relative physical fitness—were being interpreted as digs at Dave. Stockton took the stage to reiterate that this was not a war, and that his main goal for his team was to help give them memories that would last a lifetime.

But everyone knew the PGA of America had not hired David Knapp Stockton to create a memorable weekend for his team. Job one was to win back the Cup, and probably no one was better equipped to do it. Stockton had competed against the oldsters on his team—Hale, Lanny, and Raymond—but at age fifty he was not so far removed from the PGA Tour that he couldn't relate to the younger guys. Nor was he distracted by his own competitive career; not until after his captaincy would he play his first event on the over-fifty Senior PGA Tour. He had an upbeat personality and a tendency to use the word *awesome.* For almost two years, he'd been talking up the Ryder Cup to every writer and broadcaster he met. His son Dave junior was his assistant coach, and his wife, Cathy, involved herself thoroughly in details and logistics. On Thursday, Dave introduced an Official Team Song, a toe-tapping, patriotic number called "Point of Light." "If you see what's wrong/And you try to make it right," sang country music superstar Randy Travis.

"I think we were more prepared in '91," recalls O'Meara. "Stockton tried to keep it relaxed." No one on the team has a discouraging word about Dave. "He was the first modern Ryder Cup captain," says Corey Pavin. In other words, Stockton was totally absorbed by it, as Jacklin had been.

Captain Stockton's bread and butter—the corporate outing, effectively a group lesson—meant that he was a most coachlike captain. In the prime of his competitive life, he had eschewed a heavy tournament schedule in favor of about a hundred annual exhibitions and practice-tee dog-and-pony shows. ("Now, to hit a fade, I reposition the ball . . .") His main clients were Travelers Insurance, American Airlines, and, interestingly, Landmark Land, the owner of PGA West and the Ocean Course at Kiawah. From constant practice, he knew how to get his point across to leagues of extraordinary gentlemen.

"My record is not as good as it could have been had I devoted more time to my game, instead of doing so many clinics," he told Gene Wojciechowski of *PGA Magazine* in March '91. His record was nothing to be ashamed of, far from it: Stockton had won two majors, the PGA Championships of '70 and '76, and eight other events on the PGA Tour. Not that he looked all that good doing it. With the way he snatched the club up to start his stroke, and the inartistic way he came down and followed through, his swing was no one's model. But he kept it straight enough most days, and he could strategize and compete, and his Ray Cook putter had radar in it. In the *CBS Golf Classic*—a sixties and seventies TV show that was taped in the fall at Firestone Country Club in Akron—Stockton would clear tiny bits of autumn debris from the line of his putt, no matter how long it was. And then he'd make it from many yards away, or hit the lip. Amazing.

In fact, the made long putt was almost a game plan for Stockton. For example: He and Jerry McGee were two down with three to play in a 1977 Ryder Cup foursomes game against Neil Coles and Peter Dawson at Royal Lytham (this was the last of Stockton's two appearances in the Cup). On sixteen, Dave drained from forty feet to win the hole. On seventeen, he holed from fifty feet to square the match; before attempting both those putts he'd told McGee he would make them. Stunned, apparently, the balding Coles and Dawson—up to then the Ryder Cup's only left-hander—got into such a mess on eighteen that they could not finish the hole. Stockton/McGee had authored one of the Cup's greatest comebacks.

Stockton read the 1960 book *Psycho-Cybernetics* and it became his Bible. This seminal self-improvement book is easy to put down—author Maxwell Maltz had a disconcerting habit of putting quotation marks around damn near anything, and he demanded that the turgid first chapter be reread every day for three weeks.

> 1. Your built-in success mechanism must have a goal or "target." This goal, or target, must be conceived of as "already in existence—now" in actual or potential form. It operates by either (1) steering you to a goal already in existence or by (2) "discovering" something already in existence.
>
> — *Psycho-Cybernetics, page 28*

The big lesson of the book concerned the importance and malleability of self-image. You are what you think you are, in other words, and you can do what you think you can do. Those who heeded the truth of Maltz told themselves, "It would totally be like me to make this putt, or hit this green, or win this match." It was the magic of the prophecy that fulfills itself. In ways great and small, Stockton reminded his team of its objective and its ability to achieve it.

But the overall presentation and feel of the '91 Ryder Cup was less Stockton and more a blend of the perfect patriotic storm and the hopes of the PGA of America. Before the speeches about how Sportsmanship and Brotherhood and Golf were the Real Winners in the Ryder Cup, opportunities presented themselves for the U.S. side to press its home field advantage. For example: Embroidering little American flags and THE RYDER CUP BELONGS IN THE U.S. on most of the logoed merchandise brassed off European souvenir shoppers, including the European Ryder Cup team. There was that notably annoying chant: U-S-A! U-S-A! There was no counter to it. No one pulling for the other team burst into EU-ROPE! EU-ROPE! Or GER-MAN-EE! GER-MAN-EE! To Seve, the net effect "exceeded the bounds of sporting ethics. What happened at Kiawah Island was deplorable. . . . The level of aggression was something I'd never experienced in any previous outing in the Ryder Cup."

Perhaps the precise moment when Seve began to boil arrived at about nine o'clock that night, thirty-five hours before he would play in the first match. Before then, the twenty-four combatants spent the day in vigorous dress rehearsal. Two-man teams were confirmed, and hole-by-hole strategies discussed. Stewart left early with an upset stomach. Pate impressed everyone by shooting a 65; Stockton, who played in Pate's group, made a plan to use him as much as possible and to pair him with Wadkins. Two fearless guys, great scramblers who were never out of a hole? Perfect.

Virtually every player on both teams had imported his instructor to pick out tiny flaws and to say, "Looks great, great swing, stick that finish, now let's see you hit that knockdown draw." Chuck Cook (Stewart's instructor) was the highest-profile teacher on the American side; long-legged David Leadbetter (the instructor to Faldo and Seve) was the most recognizable man working with the Euros. Torrance's dad, Bob, critiqued the strokes of his son, and Feherty, and Woosnam. Sam and David challenged Seve and Olazábal to a game, and got clobbered, losing two hundred quid. At midafternoon the stars and their costars scurried back to their quarters to prepare for the social event of the week, the Gala, to be held in the elegant redbrick Omni Hotel on Meeting Street in downtown Charleston. The weather darkened.

The players and coaches of both teams put on their suits and their women wiggled into their ball gowns, then they decamped to the limos. Former UCLA teammates Pavin and Pate and their wives rode together. The Bruins must have had an incredible team in the early eighties, including as it did four future PGA Tour professionals (the other two were Tom Pernice and Jay Delsing). But they never won the NCAA, because, as Pate recalls, they never all played well at the same time.

Pate, the son of a Santa Barbara insurance man, was another player who reminded you a *little* of Ben Hogan. He played Hogan irons, for one thing, and used the same set until the chrome wore off the heads. And he shared a recessive gene with the Hawk: Competitive golf could make either of them *furious.* Hogan hid his rage with a white hat, long drags on a cigarette, and studied stoicism, but Steve's fire could not be obscured or contained. His eyes widened and whirled in extremis and his face flushed red. At least once he put an offending club behind his neck and snapped the shaft. Tee markers were smashed in two from blunt force trauma. He swore emphatically through clenched teeth. Once a college teammate asked him to keep it down; there was a lady present. "That's no lady," Pate said. "That's my mother."

When his ball finished in the orange pine straw to the right of the second fairway in the Masters at Augusta National, and his request for relief from a totally random and unfair hazard was denied—the damn thing was ten feet by ten feet!—poor Steve looked suicidal, or homicidal. In a September '99 interview with Gary Van Sickle of *Sports Illustrated*, Sheri Pate recalled walking through a tunnel at Bel-Air Country Club in Los Angeles while her crazy-mad husband repeatedly whacked the hell out of the concrete walls on both sides with one of those Hogan irons. "You name it, he's tried to stuff it into the ground," Gary McCord told Van Sickle. "Clubs, caddies, bags, everything."

Hogan found a little temper to be a useful thing. "Anger drives away fear," he said. So, too, Pate: He eventually got a deal to endorse a line of pepper sauce. Team Tabasco, they called it. "I used to stay livid for four or five hours," the Volcano said. "I could play pretty well livid, but it takes a lot of energy to stay hot that long."

But on this drizzly Wednesday night in South Carolina, the mood in the Pate/Pavin limo was anything but angry. Off the course the Volcano was a mellow fellow, with a relaxed attitude and a sly sense of humor. He had that 65 to savor, and just being on the team for the first time was reason to celebrate. After winning twice in '88, he'd been a shoo-in in '89, but he didn't have a single top ten finish from January on, and he'd missed making the team by a whisker. Now, he was in, and playing great.

●

There is no Zapruder film of the chain-reaction crash of the last three cars in the caravan, so we have to imagine it. The world's best golfers had been moving at a brisk pace through the chilling rain and dying light, running every stop sign and stoplight thanks to the strobe lights and siren blasts from the police escorts. At the county line, Charleston city cops took over the motorcade. The cars slowed to about twenty miles per hour; rain fell; headlights glared off the shiny pavement; rush hour traffic stood aside.

At 7:38 EST, Feherty's wife, Caroline, distracted their limo driver with a question. He hit the brakes. Screech, clink, crash, as three sets of grilles and headlights met bumpers. One occupant of the middle car got the worst of it—Pate. He flew through the air and "hit the front seat on my side," he says. "I wound up on the floor, sideways. I knew it wasn't good." Shannon Pavin had a banged-up elbow but only Steve was really hurt.

Elder statesmen Floyd and Irwin accompanied their fallen comrade to Bon Secours–Saint Francis Xavier Hospital and kept Stockton apprised by phone. A quick X-ray of the important and well-dressed patient revealed no broken bones; Ray and Hale joined the party at the Omni, while Pate stayed behind to receive treatment. Kerry Haigh—the course setup man for the PGA of America—stayed behind with the quiescent Volcano. They would return to Kiawah after midnight. The upshot was that dinner was more than an hour late and its tone had turned somber.

Stage managers had Team Europe walk in first. They acknowledged the applause and took tables on the side. Team USA entered to louder cheering from the home diners. They took the tables in the center. "They were in the thick of things," Montgomerie recalled. "We were on the outskirts and feeling like outsiders. Needless to say, there were some discontented mutterings."

Bruised feelings were assuaged with California wine; Romaine Salad with Julienne of Tri-Colored Peppers, Toasted Croutons, and Parmesan Peppercorn Dressing; Layered Seafood Terrine with Papaya Chile Relish; and Medallions of Veal with Pesto Cream. There were a couple of brief speeches, some autographing. At the Gala dinner in England two years before, Captain Raymond Floyd had needlessly provoked the opposition by introducing his squad as "the twelve greatest players in the world"—borrowing the phrase from Hogan, when he presented his Ryder Cup team in 1947. But the shoe didn't fit in 1989; Seve and Faldo and Langer and Woosnam had among them won more majors than the U.S. team combined. Faldo whispered to Captain Jacklin that he should stand and introduce Seve as the thirteenth-best player in the world.

How would the U.S. side screw up the evening this time? With a video.

Just as spoons were dipping into desserts, PGA of America president Dick Smith introduced an NBC production entitled

"A History of the Ryder Cup." Tape rolled on a couple of giant screens. The twenty-minute presentation was laughably, heavy-handedly pro-U.S.; there was nothing in it from the recent glory years for Europe. There were Arnold and Jack and Lee and Watson making putts and grinning hero's grins—but no Seve, no Sir Henry Cotton, no Christy O'Connor, no Torrance.

"Shameful!" cried out European PGA Tour director Ken Schofield. He and a few others in the official party made as to leave. Montgomerie whispered incredulously to Eimear. Seve muttered—"*¡Esto es mierda!*" perhaps. Sarcasm from others . . . after the video, Gallacher took the stage to introduce his team, making no reference to the propaganda film just exhibited. Lanny approached Bernard afterward to say he hoped a letter of apology would be forthcoming.

The Gatlin Brothers Band cut their postdinner show to just a few songs, and the party broke up. There were questions for the forty-five-minute ride back to Kiawah. Would Stockton call his leading nonqualifier, Tim Simpson, to fly in to take Pate's place? Could you believe that movie? Think Faldo will learn how to putt by Friday? Will that bunghole of a disc jockey try to wake everyone again?

9

THURSDAY, SEPTEMBER 26

On days when the Ryder Cup was not in residence, the view from the Ocean Course clubhouse was unique in golf: One beheld a broad, flat plain, a thousand yards long and perhaps two hundred yards wide, about right for a polo match. Beyond the acres of green trimmed with white stood stiff beige stalks of sea grass on sand dunes. Beyond that, the beach, and the infinite sea.

The golf course lay on either side of the polo pitch: first nine left, back nine right. The Ocean Course had its inspirations but no real precedent; it looked as if it had been designed by René Magritte, the Belgian surrealist painter who made it rain men with umbrellas. It was beautiful. It was impossible. And in the center of Dye's acres of whorls and vortices that blank space was a punctuation mark, a hard stop halfway through the journey. The vastness between the ninth green and tenth tee meant that there would be a front-nine crowd and a second-nine crowd. Those who wished to watch a match continuously would have to scurry from the ninth to the eleventh or twelfth hole. Players and caddies were, naturally, carted from nine to ten.

The Opening Ceremony took place on the practice ground. After a final practice round—Langer made a hole in one on seventeen, and Ballesteros/Olazábal easily beat Faldo/Woosnam, which made Nick and Ian visibly unhappy—the impressive formal opening began. Peter Jacobsen, a gifted mimic and comedian, loosened up the crowd with his golf swing impersonations. His Palmer included Arnie reaching into his shirt to pull out a tuft of chest hair, which he tossed into the air to test the wind. Jacobsen's Trevino, Gary Player, and Craig Stadler (a large basket of golf balls poured into his shirt simulated the Stadler gut) also reliably drew laughs. To do Ray Floyd—the only Ryder Cupper on his playlist—Jake yanked the club back abruptly inside, then picked it up to his right ear, executing the entire unusual stroke with Raymond's dancelike tempo. And then he did the Ray walk, with its peculiar short stride.

Speeches began. "Another great chapter of sportsmanship and play [in] the history of the Ryder Cup," said Jacklin. Eminences were recognized, such as Deane Beman of the PGA Tour, and Chris Cole, president of Kiawah Island Golf and Tennis, who was also the general chairman for the '91 Ryder Cup. There was a drill team from The Citadel; an ear-splitting, low-altitude flyby of four South Carolina Air National Guard F-16 jets, each piloted by a Gulf War veteran (the Gulf War references now starting to annoy the soul out of Team Europe); an eleven-minute performance by the twenty-four-man U.S. Marine Corps Silent Drill Platoon; bagpipes; the national anthems of each country represented. The American wives entered, dressed in identical star-spangled red, white, and blue sweaters, and waving little American flags. The European wives wore mufti.

The tide was out; you could see beach walkers oblivious to golf and any so-called war on this shore. The two captains marched in side by side in the glorious afternoon sunshine—with Gallacher carrying the Ryder Cup—and behind them the twenty-four players, each opposite a member of the opposing team, every one of them smiling and handsome and twenty-odd years younger than now. Blue blazers and gray slacks for Europe, cream-colored sport coats and khaki for the USA. Gallacher introduced his players with full orchestration and five-part harmony; Stockton was far less effusive.

The first-round pairings were announced, to applause. Past success and close friendship removed any doubt about the makeup of most of the two-man teams (two vs. two would be the game all day Friday and Saturday, singles on Sunday). That meant Seve and Olly, Nick and Woosie, and Torrance and Feherty. Floyd had been brought in, in part, to team with Couples; Beck would be reprising his role as Azinger's sidekick. After that, Captain Stockton had problems. Steve Pate loved the drama of match play, and he'd been playing so well that Stockton might have used him in five matches, the maximum. Now, no one knew if he'd be able to play at all, and Dave wasn't going to bring in a replacement this late in the game. Levi needed hiding; he hadn't played well all year, and he hadn't suddenly clicked into gear this week. O'Meara's back was iffy.

Furthermore, O'Meara and Stewart—to Lanny's great disgust—had both declined to be paired with Hale Irwin. There was an age gap (Hale was forty-six, and Mark and Payne were both thirty-four) but the bigger divide lay in their personalities. Irwin, an All–Big 8 defensive back at Colorado back in the day, brought football attitude with him onto the course, and it helped him win three U.S. Opens. He intimidated opponents—including, apparently, Mark and Payne.

"What wimps," says Wadkins. "I told them, 'He'll be on *your* team. What have you got to worry about?' So I said, 'I'll take him.' Shit, who wouldn't want Hale Irwin?"

Which team would win?

One reasonable but unhelpful analysis simply looked at the World Golf Rankings. Europe had numbers one through four plus seven (their end-of-the-year rankings in 1991 were, in order, Woosnam, Faldo, Olazábal, Seve, and Langer) so they had greater star power. The Americans owned greater depth, with Couples, Stewart, and Azinger in the top ten, and every member of the team in the top forty. Which side was more motivated? The spurs in the sides of the Yanks were plain. According to those of us with a pen, in recent bouts the U.S. team had resembled an undertrained and overweight boxer, without the heart to rise to the challenge of a determined foe. But on Thursday, September 26, 1991, it seemed fit to fight. "We got beat up pretty bad when we lost, which I didn't really appreciate," recalls O'Meara. "No one gave a crap until we started to lose. I'm still a little resentful."

Team Europe's incentive—simplifying a bit—was to prove with temporary finality that it had the better players, the better tour, the superior captain.[1] No one would dare doubt it if not for the amazing rally by the United States in '89 that had salvaged a tie. McCumber, Watson, Wadkins, and Strange had taken the last four singles matches.

Which team would win? The Ryder Cup had lately been supplying delicious examples of literature's three great themes: man against man, man against nature, man against himself. It would come down to individuals, in other words, as golf always does.

In the first match in the morning, sunshine would be playing midnight. It would be the nicest guy you've ever met against the dark, indignant genius from Pedreña.

1 Speaking *en español* to the Spanish press, Seve said this Ryder Cup wasn't any war, "it's only a competition between two continents to prove which is better."

PART THREE
EL JUEGO

Golf should be more like pro wrestling. Wouldn't it be great if a guy was standing over a birdie putt and you could just go over and deck him, absolutely flatten him? Man, I'd pay to see that.

—*Paul Azinger, to* Sports Illustrated *writer John Garrity, in a 1990 interview*

THE STAKES

Sports psychologist Lanny Bassham uses an uncomplicated metaphor to illustrate how raising the stakes can make even a simple task difficult. Bassham asks his students to imagine a ten-foot-long, four-inch beam lying flat on the floor. If I bet a hundred dollars that you can't walk across that beam without falling, the former Olympic gold medal winner asks, would you take it? Everyone nods his head. Of course; easy money.

But what if I put that same girder a hundred feet in the air, Bassham wonders, how many of you would accept my wager now?

When the conscious mind takes over actions that have been shaped by endless practice into instinct, tasks that have seemed so easy—hitting a drive with a little draw, holing an uphill putt of five feet, walking in a straight line—can seem harder than irregular verbs in Bengali. "No one *dies* from a bad shot," points out Dan Strimple, the well-known Dallas-based golf instructor. "Knowing the true cost of failure can free you to perform to your potential." Which is true enough, usually—but playing in the Ryder Cup had become the equivalent of dancing on beams high above the ground . . . in spiked shoes. Failure in this curious rivalry loomed as a kind of living death, destined to be revisited every other year into eternity.

The Media 700 assembled in the big tent collectively neglected to examine the psychological implications in their pregame analyses. Someone surely might have thought to wonder if athletes under extreme duress tend more to strive toward glory or instead hunker down in hope of avoiding disgrace. Framing the question in such a black-and-white way ignores the complexity of the reality the players faced, but at least it would suggest the potential train wreck looming around the bend. The pressure arrived in thousands of sensory inputs: the sound of surf and seabirds; the presence of their anxious wives; the flapping of nylon national flags held by very intent spectators; the gallery breaking into *chants*, for God's sake; the millions of electronic watchers signified by the TV cameras locked onto every shot of every match; and the Greek chorus of walking experts murmuring into radio and TV microphones. Above all was the petrifying responsibility of playing not just for a team, but for a country or a continent, on a field of play with minuscule margins for error.

But we didn't think about thinking in 1991 as much as we do these days. We hadn't pondered the notion of emotional intelligence, for example. We knew that the subconscious ran our automatic systems like breathing and blinking and that a vigilant conscious mind was nominally in control of whether we ordered pancakes or scrambled eggs. Freud's idea of the three-part psyche—impulsive id, responsible ego, judgmental superego—had been around since 1923, but it was taking its place alongside Marxism in the museum of obsolete ideas.

But other ways of understanding the supercomputer lolling on top of our necks were coming to light. "The brain is a team of rivals," writes neuroscientist David Eagleman in his 2011 book *Incognito: The Secret Lives of the Brain*. "Behavior is the outcome of the battle among internal systems." The conscious mind, writes Eagleman, is in fact far less important or in charge of how we behave than once thought. And sometimes the brain's teeming democracy of nanocomputers cannot agree. Sometimes the little weenie at the helm asks for the impossible, like a low, hooking one-iron into a left-to-right crosswind that lands gently in the few square yards between a lagoon and a bunker as big as a whale's grave after you've been hitting fades all day—all year!—and while twenty thousand people breathe down your neck and Johnny Miller whispers into a microphone connected to millions and millions of TVs.

Over the last two decades, behaviorists and brain scientists have learned a lot about the concept that in sports is summarized with one simple word: *choke*. Modern neuroscience may not have much to offer in terms of therapies, but it has given us insight into everything from impulse purchases to failed diets to addictions. The more we know about the brain, the less we seem in charge of our own destinies. Yet we assume our surrogate warriors in the arena can control their fates with willpower and dedication.

Instead of musing about the electrical signals inside the golfers' skulls, the writers interviewed each other for predictions of who would win. Renton Laidlaw of the London *Evening Standard* and BBC Radio picked Europe. Jaime Diaz of *The New York Times* voted for the United States. Mitchell Platts, of the London *Times*, foresaw a three-point victory for Europe. "This course is so tough, no match is going to go to eighteen," predicted Tim Rosaforte of *The Palm Beach Post*. "Maybe that's why they didn't build bleachers there."

The players went to bed, hoping for sleep, and woke up early with rosy fingers around their necks. The bugle call for the most dramatic golf event ever was about to sound.

10

FRIDAY MORNING, SEPTEMBER 27

In the days before the competition, Kerry Haigh of the PGA of America and George Frye of Kiawah had strolled the Ocean Course with Pete Dye, getting the architect's thoughts on how the holes should play, the goal being to maximize the challenge for the players without actually making them walk off the course blubbering. The players knew Dye wouldn't mind visiting a little humiliation on their delicate psyches, but hoped Haigh and Frye would help protect their self-esteem.

The principal tool in their kit was the speed of the greens—they'd be moderately fast, they decided, nothing crazy; 10.5 on the Stimp—but with those fun-house hills and valleys, and the likelihood of strong wind, ten-five could be like ice. Where they'd set the pins and place the tee markers were the final variables. But the setup men knew they didn't know what they were doing, because of the unpredictable breezes at Kiawah. All week holes one through five going out and the last five coming in had played downwind, but as the first group came to the first tee, the four combatants felt a breeze in their faces. How inconvenient! Up ahead, Haigh and a maintenance crew under the direction of Superintendent Steve Miller raced to amend the locations of the tee markers and of the four-and-a-half-inch-wide holes in the ground. Dye's definite preference was to keep the markers back on holes into the wind, and make 'em play *really* long.

Eight o'clock A.M.: Ding—ding—ding—ding! With the way this contest was playing out, it's not that big of a stretch to imagine the hammer on the brass bell, the lowering microphone, and tuxedoed ring announcer Michael Buffer stepping into the sun to do his Let's Get Ready to Rumble thing. "WELCOME, ladies and gentlemen, to the 1991 Ryder Cup! The first four matches will be foursomes—that's alternate shot to you and me! In the blue corner: the champions. Representing Europe, wearing white shirts, brick-red trousers, and dark blue sleeveless pullovers, with a Ryder Cup team record of six wins, one defeat, and one tie—the almost Unbeatable Basques, José María Olazábal and Severiano Ballesteros, the Spanish ARMA-DA!" Applause. Olazábal hit first—a bullet down the middle with his brown MacGregor persimmon driver.

More imaginary ruffles and flourishes from the bombastic Buffer: "And in the red corner: the challengers. Representing the United States of America, wearing white shirts, navy-blue slacks, and red short-sleeved pullovers . . . as rookies they were America's only UNDEFEATED[1] tandem at the 1989 Ryder

1 They were 2-0.

Cup. They're the team with no nickname—yet!—Mr. A and Mr. B—Paul Azinger and Chip Beck!"

Louder applause, and Beck addressed his 90 compression Titleist ball with a TaylorMade metal three-wood. He swung and stared as his ball drifted right, off the side of the raised fairway and into the sand border. Stockton watched solemnly. Given the testy history between Paul and Seve, the U.S. captain had hoped to keep them apart, but the two unusually fierce competitors would be hitting from the same tees all morning.

Would Olazábal and Beck help keep the atmosphere civil? José María had no reputation for confrontation, but in the team milieu he deferred to Seve. Chip owned the most upbeat personality in the hemisphere. You could make him take a long walk with Glenn Beck (no relation) or a Kardashian or whatever annoying person you can think of and Chip would have him or her smiling all day. Some pros find it hard to even pretend to be interested in their partners in the weekly Wednesday pro-am, but Beck would make four new friends for life. He'd do shtick. "Raise your head and hold it high/Chip Beck's group is passing by!" he sang like a happy drill instructor. He gave lessons. "Stand up to that ball! With a posture like that, the club weighs seventy pounds!" He got down on his hands and knees and buffed the mud off the shoes of his amazed teammates. You busy for dinner, Chip? the amateurs asked. We're buying! Here's how he handled Azinger:

"There'd be a bad crosswind and a narrow patch of fairway between two bunkers, and he'd say, 'I think I can hit a driver in there.' So I'd say, 'Zinger, you go ahead and hit that driver.' "

The Armada and Azinger-Beck tied the first hole with pars—Azinger was not conceded an eighteen-inch putt. The bickering began about six minutes later. On the second hole the golfer had to fly over significant trouble twice while avoiding it on either side. Against the wind the prospect of the long par five was so discouraging that a casual player might think of going back to his room, or to the beach, or to the ladies' tees. Seve hit a horrid pull-hook into the marsh on the left. Zinger's turn: A European writer had referred to him as "some sort of stick insect" but he looked less so this week. He'd put on fifteen pounds during the inactivity following shoulder surgery and the extra weight looked good on him. Paul swung his slap shot of a swing and drilled it into the fairway. After a fruitless search in the thigh-high swamp grass—the Americans did not join the search party—Seve wanted Olly to drop well up the fairway. Paul said no way, you've got to drop back there.

Unpleasantness already.

A few minutes later Chip holed an eight-footer for birdie four—Seve/Olly had already conceded the hole, and would have had an 8 or 9 if they'd holed out. Team U.S. was one-up in match one.

Soon after this little flare-up, Paul began to annoy by standing as close as a nongolfing girlfriend on Seve's subsequent shots from the rough or near hazards—or so Seve remembers it. "*¡Qué tío tan torpe!*" said Seve in rapid Castilian to his teammate, whom he had nicknamed Chema. "*Siempre está observando mi pelota y se para un metro.... está muy preocupado de que yo le vaya a ganar.*"

In English: "What an awkward so-and-so, always watching

my ball from a meter away. He's very worried that I'm going to kick his ass in this match." A loose translation, but that was the drift.

Chip and José María let their partners do the talking and the posturing. Beck had grown up in the next state north, where people watching what they eat were said to be on a dot, and that thing on top of your head is a Hyatt. The third oldest of the ten children of a Fayetteville dentist, little Chip picked up a club for the first time at age ten, and was winning junior tournaments by the end of the year. After a big-time college golf career at the University of Georgia, he happily faced the long series of road games that is the bedrock of professional golf, his uplifting demeanor derived equally from a genetic gift and from the joy he felt in his Roman Catholic faith.

His golf instructor was Ray Floyd's dad, who reached the summit of his profession one hot June Sunday on Long Island. That was the day his forty-three-year-old baby boy won the 1986 U.S. Open at Shinnecock Hills, and Chip, sprinting to the finish with 68-65, finished tied for second with Lanny. Beck saw L. B. Floyd afterward, an old man in a wheelchair with a tear in his eye. "This is the greatest day of my life," Floyd senior said.

After more grim adventures, the teams halved the fiendish par-four fourth in double bogey, with Seve holing from fifteen feet for the six. But during the hole there had been another protest from Zinger regarding the location of the drop after another wild drive by Seve. At five, the course turned back toward the clubhouse and the players finally felt the wind at their backs. By the beach now; the tide was in. Beck hit his ball on the green on the par three, while Seve missed the surface. The United States won par to bogey and went two-up. At about this time Gallacher learned via the radios he and his surrogates had been given that his team trailed in all four matches. And then he discovered that his radio was on an open channel; anyone from Dave Stockton to the truckers on Highway 17 could listen in. Not sporting.

Intelligence from the battlefield was vital, because the captains would be required to turn in their rosters for the afternoon fourball one hour before the end of the morning matches. They wanted to know how each player was handling himself, not just the scores of their matches. For strategic purposes, the comments should have been private.[2]

Pars halved the sixth. Beck looked frustrated with the steady accumulation of can-you-believe-this? missed putts. He was not used to it. When most golfers get a few under par, their focus switches subtly from offense to defense. But Beck had spent the entirety of 1988 in red numbers, winning the Vardon Trophy for low stroke average on the PGA Tour. And a month after this Ryder Cup, in a tournament round in Las Vegas, he would birdie thirteen of eighteen holes for a 59, only the second 59 in PGA Tour history. But today, nothing.

The four combatants had so much in common. What was their main difference, besides their addresses? Maybe what they'd done

2 Gallacher's suspicions were confirmed on Sunday, when he moaned into his radio about the impossibility of following all of the singles matches—and Stockton's voice piped in, assuring him that he could do it. Whoops.

from their mid-teens to their early twenties was a real point of differentiation. The Americans were all college boys. Beck, the Georgia Bulldog, got a BA in Journalism. Azinger went to Brevard Community College in Cocoa, and Florida State (briefly). Same basic deal with the rest of Team USA, except that Floyd barely kept a seat warm in his quick pass through the University of North Carolina.

The Europeans, on the other hand, followed the ancient path trod by Old Tom and Sam Snead: from caddie to pro. Seve gave up the books forever at age fifteen, while Olly was a touring pro at age nineteen. The more worldly Euros knew the best hotel in Saint-Nom-la-Bretèche and how to order a steak in four languages, while the Yanks had had time to contemplate the big picture in Philosophy 101. But it was the supposedly better-educated group that suddenly went brain-dead in this match. As Beck explained in 2011, "We just forgot."

On the seventh tee, Olazábal overheard the Americans discussing which ball to play. Should they use Beck's 90 compression—which spun more but didn't go as far as Azinger's 100? In theory, the 90 might hold the green better, while the 100 had a better chance of going the distance on the downwind, 578-yard hole. They didn't have an option, of course. On odd holes they had to use Chip's brand. But they used Paul's ball. On the next hole, the eighth, José María whispered into his partner's ear about what the Americans were up to. Hadn't they read the Rules sheet? Didn't they remember the Rules meeting? And were they breaking the Rule on this hole and would they do it again on the next?

"San! San!" Seve gestured urgently to Sam Torrance—who

was watching this match before his own in the afternoon, and whose name Seve never got quite right. "Big problem. San, get Bernard now. Big problem." San—Sam—couldn't raise the captain on the radio; rather than reveal anything to prying ears, Gallacher had switched the damn thing off. Torrance absquatulated. The teams tied holes seven and eight. On nine, a 463-yard par four, architect Dye asked the golfer for a hook off the tee, but Olly hit a push into the lagoon on *el derecho*. Azinger watched with sharp eyes as his opponents were about to drop. Not again. No, no *way*, Paul said. Not there. Back *there*. He called for the law, a serious escalation.

Players can almost always agree among themselves on such things, but not these players, not on this day.

"I was livid," recalled Zinger, writing about it four years later. "The referee was intimidated by Seve and José. . . . We argued over it for a while, and finally Seve looked at me with disgust and said, 'Okay, where do you want me to drop it?' "

Team Europe bogeyed nine, the finishing touch on a front nine of 40; Team America parred it, to go three-up. Or did it? Now the party really started. Behind the green, Gallacher—he'd been briefed by "San" Torrance—joined with the four players and the match referee and the chief referee, Larry Startzel. The discussion regarding ball switching convened after the thousand-yard golf cart journey to the tenth tee.

"Seve was fuming."—Torrance

"I was furious!"—Azinger

"Shows what the Spaniards knew about the rules—they waited so they could try to claim three holes."—Lanny

The tenth tee at the Ocean perched atop a sand dune, providing a panoramic view of the back nine and the ocean as well as a theater in the round for TV cameras and for spectators. Eyewitnesses—an Ocean Course caddie; a reporter; a dentist from High Point, North Carolina—recall a dismaying spectacle of finger pointing, red faces, and dramatic gesturing. "It was very heated," recalls the journalist. "I couldn't believe it. The next step would have been pushing."

The videotape does not bear out the eyewitness memories, but there may have been emotional fury the cameras could not capture. The golfers, their arms crossed, seemed more like angry but polite motorists in the wake of a fender bender, pleading their cases to the cop. For long minutes the debate raged. Alternately defiant and conciliatory, Azinger would not admit to any wrongdoing. Rules expert Startzel, a club pro from Florida, sorted out the facts. The players in the following match arrived on the scene, but Floyd and Couples and James and Langer just watched along with everyone else. Azinger kept saying that he and Chip had no intention to cheat. Startzel echoed Dan Rather during Watergate: What did you know, and when did you know it? Did you, Seve and Olly, bring up the alleged breach on the seventh hole before the teams teed off on the eighth? No? Then, according to Rule 2-5, there is no penalty. At this point, Azinger admitted that he and Chip *had* switched golf balls on seven; so the real issue was nine. If it had been a good idea for Chip to drive with Paul's ball on seven, wasn't it still a good idea on nine, another long hole playing downwind?

Azinger: "We played Chip's ball, the correct one, on nine."

Chema and Seve: "We're sure you played the wrong ball on seven, eight, and nine. We heard you talking about it."

Finally, Gallacher stepped in and told his boys to play on. No penalty was assessed. The discussion had lasted about fifteen minutes. It was 10:40.

"Well, we're certainly not cheating," Azinger said again. "No, no," said Olly and Seve, almost in unison. "We didn't say that." And Seve is supposed to have jabbed the air with an indignant finger and said, "Cheating and ignorance of the Rules are two different things."[3] But things looked peaceful, if not harmonious, as Paul, then Seve, hit iron shots down the tenth fairway.

Why was Severiano Ballesteros so frequently affronted by the world generally and by Azinger in particular? His peers and the press insisted that Seve simply loved to beat Americans, as if this could explain his accomplishment. His gaudy success in the Masters (seven times in the top five, including two wins) proved that he was a great player on American dirt, but he also won three Open Championships, and no one ever accused him of despising Brits. Despite winning only one point and losing four in his first Ryder Cup in '79, Seve won twice as often as he lost thereafter (his career win-loss-tie numbers would be 20-12-5). The truth was, Seve enjoyed beating anyone and everyone at any time. (Witness his fifty wins—the most

3 A month later, at the Volvo Masters in Spain, Seve gave an interview that was picked up by every major paper in the United States. "Azinger didn't cheat," he said, "but he lied. He said it [the ball change] happened only once, but we know it happened three times. At first he denied it completely, then when he realized they could not lose the hole he changed his statement. He was the only one of the American team that did not behave in a proper manner. The American team were eleven nice guys and Paul Azinger."

ever—on the Volvo European PGA Tour.) But in his view, taking down U.S. players exalted Spain, his family, Pedreña, and the Continent, and Seve cared about such things.

There was an origin myth favored by advocates of the Seve-hates-America theory: the Steve Story. In Woosnam's version, the culprit was a dolt of an American fan hanging around the hotel on the eve of the 1985 Ryder Cup. Some say the ignoramus was a chipper American TV interviewer.

"I'm here with sensational Spanish golfer Steve Ball A-stare-ose. Steve, tell us about your round today. . . ." Seve vented to friends afterward. "He calls me Steve. Steve? Who is this fucking Steve?"

The one-ball brouhaha concluded, but it had only lifted the intensity of the match. Paul went too hard for the birdie putt on ten, and Chip missed the resultant five-footer. Europe had a steady par and was now two down. "Let's play the back nine really well," Seve recalled in *Seve*. "Whatever they do, we're going to beat them."

And Olazábal believed him. Like a great coach, Seve could inspire. "Look what he did with Piñero in '85!" says former European Tour executive director Ken Schofield. "Seve could lift any teammate up." Manuel Piñero could play the game, all right, but his talent and accomplishment hovered far below that of Langer, Woosnam, or Faldo. Yet Piñero paired with Ballesteros won three of four at the Belfry in the Great Upset.

Perhaps Seve's knack for moving a mate to exceed himself was a component of his legendary magnetism, the charisma that seemed to infuse the air as he swung a club (harder than anyone else) or marched down a fairway (or more dramatically, into the trees; Seve's forte was the recovery shot from an impossible quandary).

Most great performers are zip-lipped and closed off—nothing wrong with that—because tournament golf requires a lot of heavy mental lifting. Who emotes during the bar exam, or the history final? But the last half century gave us two world-class golfers so emotive and engaging that they swept innocent bystanders into their drama. Arnold Palmer and the man from Pedreña drew the eye like a diamond on a beige rug. Not for nothing was Seve called the Arnie of Europe. Someone wrote long ago that Ballesteros was a matador, and golf was his bull.

One of the TV boys collared Gallacher and asked him about the debate on the tenth tee. Captain Bernard responded with a terse summary. "And how do you think the matches are going?" asked Mick Luckhurst, who should have known better. Europe trailed in all four. "Very quickly," said Gallacher, who then broke TV protocol by simply walking away.

The teams halved the eleventh in par. Dye's succinct scouting report for the twelfth, a 466-yard par four: "Miss it right or left [off the tee] and it's a disaster." Seve hit a strong drive in the fairway; Azinger prepared to play. And then it happened:

Just as the slender, intense American initiated his launch sequence, Seve coughed. Zinger backed off, and stared laser beams at his antagonist. A minute later José María bounced a brilliant second shot almost in the hole. The United States was now just one up.

Memoirs may be the traditional vehicle for coming clean, but Seve played the innocent regarding this incident. "I often cough and sneeze because I have allergies," he wrote. "But Azinger looked at me as if I'd done it on purpose." Hadn't he? The tickle in the Ballesteros throat had cropped up often enough. He stayed alert for gamesmanship in others and gave it back more than once. When Tom Watson urged him to hit first to the fifteenth green at Augusta National, when he, Watson, was away—Seve thought this a ploy. While the tickle in his throat occurred often enough to have a name—his "educated cough"—*el señor* unashamedly employed other gambits that were not cheating but might give him an advantage.

For example: On this same day, against this same high-strung opponent, Seve chipped to about a meter from the hole while Zinger's ball was practically a tap-in. The Spaniard suggested that they concede the putts to each other—a "good-good"—a preposterous idea that Azinger rejected. But for Seve, the payoff was worth the ruse. He was just trying to get inside Zinger's head. As he recalled in *Seve*, "To stress him more I added, 'But I'm putting first.' "

On thirteen at the Ocean, the green seemed unhinged from the land, so far right did it jut into the marsh. Seve stuck the iron shot this time, a nine iron from 136 yards, and Olly rolled in the five-footer. Match even. The course did a 180 at this point, so the final five played alongside the beach and into the freshening wind. The sun approached its midpoint in the pale blue sky.

When in 1936 Generalísimo Francisco Franco fomented a coup against Spain's democratically elected Republican government, it launched a brutal civil war. The Republicans drafted Baldomero Ballesteros into the army. But Seve's father employed an ancient tactic to avoid service with the leftist government he despised. Taking up his Republican gun, he fired a shot through his own left hand, a pure expression of passive-aggression. He was sentenced to twenty years but escaped from the hospital and found his way to the front, where he fought with Franco's rebels until war's end. The general borrowed Hitler's air force and bombed a Basque town, Guernica, a strategy the Nazis would use a few years later on civilian targets in Poland, Czechoslovakia, and Belgium. The destruction in Seve's Basque homeland is memorialized in history's most famous antiwar painting, Picasso's *Guernica.*

Back home after the war, Baldomero and the former Carmen Sota settled into a tranquil life. They grew corn, beets, beans, potatoes, and greens; dug on the beach for *morgueras* (shellfish); and they raised fourteen milk cows and four sons. There might have been five boys, but the firstborn, Manuel, died as an infant from bee stings. No one in the family was allowed to forget Manuel's death, and thus, his own mortality.

Pedreña sat on the northern rim of Spain, in the Basque country between the Bay of Biscay and the Cantabrian Mountains. Neither Madrid nor Barcelona, themselves historic rivals, could accept Basque autonomy. Seve had Basque in his blood and his bones. His ancestors were insular, with culture, traditions, and even religion distinct from the rest of Spain. Don't think Amish or Mormons or Norwegians in America; they were more separate than that, and more capable of violence in their struggle to remove themselves from Spanish rule. For decades underground Basque terrorist groups closely resembling the IRA ignited bombs and discharged weapons in a fruitless effort to gain independence.

But Basque separatism was far from Seve's mind growing up. His unprepossessing hometown was a peaceful place, containing nothing but a few hundred subsistence farmers and their stone houses and barns, plus a church, a pharmacy, one telephone, three bars, and, oddly, a golf course. Seve and brother Vicente looked over the fence as they grazed the cows in a field next to Royal Club of Pedreña. Curiosity about the wealthy men and their stick-and-ball game—and a strong desire to earn a few pesetas—led to caddying. And soon Seve was channeling Sam Snead. A first club was a stick driven into a discarded three-iron head.[4] The little boy whacked rocks on the beach with *el tres*, and then actual balls, lost-and-found or stolen. Sneaking on the forbidden golf course, playing it by moonlight or in dim starlight, he acquired an aspirational feeling toward golf, and a permanent slight resentment toward its gatekeepers. And one other thing: Like Jack Nicklaus, Seve developed a deep understanding of golf as *a game, un juego,* not

4 Seve had ample precedents in his family for making a life in golf. All three of his older brothers became professionals, and his mother's brother was Ramón Sota, the winner of the Dutch, French, Portuguese, Spanish, Puerto Rican, and Italian Opens. Tío Ramón also finished T-7 in the '63 Open Championship, and T-6 in the Masters in '65. But Sota appears not to have helped his nephew with, for example, some free clubs and balls. "There wasn't much communication between us," wrote Seve. "Ramón was very withdrawn."

as a hard-edged science with schematics of swing planes, and certainly not as a vehicle to satisfy a parent's desire for him to participate in something rather than play video games all summer. With his caddie DNA, the confrontation and vagaries of match play suited him particularly.

●

While Seve's instinct for improvisation and his nose for the finish line won many matches, it also helped to have a great partner. Fourteen, halved in pars. On fifteen, a 468-yard par four playing 520, with a green blended into the end of a rolling fairway, Olazábal drove into the sand right, then Seve whacked it into the sand left. The Americans, on the green in two, seemed poised to go back ahead. But José María blasted out to three feet, a wonderful shot, and Azinger and Beck contrived to three-putt.

Team Europe took the lead, and won the match, two holes later, on the diabolical seventeenth. Olly and Beck both hit very good shots to the scary target. Azinger missed his putt. Seve, from about twenty-five feet, did not. Every other game in the morning would go to the U.S. team. The win by Seve/Olly was therefore surpassingly important, for no side had ever been shut out in the first series and come back to win the Match.

There were hard feelings. In the presence of people with pens and notebooks, Zinger referred to Seve as "the king of gamesmanship." Stockton hadn't wanted these two together to start with, and he surely didn't want a reprise of coughs and recriminations in the afternoon match. Assuming that Gallacher would again put his top team out first, Captain Dave slid his top two—Beck and Azinger—into the second afternoon match. But Bernard decided to give Seve/Olly a longish rest, and assigned them the second match too. Paul and Chip would be battling the Spanish Armada again in the afternoon. *Caramba.*

Friday Morning Results: USA 3, Europe 1
Ballesteros/Olazábal defeated Azinger/Beck 2 and 1
Floyd/Couples defeated James/Langer 2 and 1

Reacting either to the slight chill in the air or to the strange buildup of excitement in his body, the normally placid Couples jumped up and down on the first tee as if he were on a pogo stick. "Teeing off for the European team," began a PGA of America man in a sport coat and a hundred-dollar haircut. The ursine James walked with his weight slightly forward, and with minimal arm swing. He would have had to cheer up to look glum. Langer surprised by not using his usual grip for a five-foot putt for par and a tie on the first hole. He used the split cross-hand, but did not hold his left forearm and the putter in the same embrace. He hit a good putt, but it missed.

USA Network ran a recorded interview with Fred's elderly partner. "The wonderful thing about this Ryder Cup is I'm playing beautifully," Floyd said. "I'm playing as good as I ever have in my career. I feel like I'm twenty-five or -six years old."

Golfers seldom emit such sunshine, preferring instead to fret a bit about the long irons or a sore latissimus dorsi. But the forty-nine-year-old Floyd—the player who had once been a Ryder Cup captain—exuded enthusiasm and energy for the little things, like congratulating Couples. And putting: After three quarters of a four-up lead disappeared, Raymundo holed from six feet for par on fifteen to stay one hole ahead, and he scored from eight feet on sixteen—again for par—to win the hole. Couples nailed a three iron on the 197-yard seventeenth. "What a golf shot! What a golf shot!" chirped Raymond while the ball arced over the lagoon and toward the hidden pin. Floyd lagged within an inch or two for the par and the win.

The howling wind made the final five play *very* hard. Langer, a shorter hitter than Couples, had used a six iron for his ace on seventeen the day before. "I finally won a Ryder Cup match," said Fred, who'd been 0-2 in '89. His mate, Deborah, danced out onto the green, a grinning, vivid figure with big earrings, prominent teeth, and blond-streaked hair.

Wadkins/Irwin vs. Gilford/Montgomerie

They'd worked it out the day before, when Stockton gave them the pairings: Hale would drive on the odd-numbered holes, Lanny the evens. But just as the man with the mic announced his name, and as the gallery applauded, Irwin whispered to his partner: "I can't hit this shot. You take it." Wadkins gave him a what-the-hell? look, then subbed in and struck his usual low screamer down the middle.[5]

That the moment had overwhelmed a man only fourteen months removed from his third U.S. Open win speaks more to the incredible buildup and pressure than it does to any weakness in Hale—who hit the second shot on one to within five feet of the hole, and the third shot on two to within a foot. Wadkins made the putts, the team went four-up through six, and the Old Masters never let the Euro rookies up for air. Colin/David seemed sure to win the ninth, for example, when Irwin blew the second shot way over the green, into the scrub, and under the stout arms of coastal oak. Lanny contorted himself into a squat, made a left-handed jab at the ball with his brass-headed Acushnet Bulls Eye putter, and watched it hop out in a puff of sand and roll up onto the green. Irwin holed the fifteen-footer for a tie that felt like a win. Colin/David extended the match to the sixteenth hole, then they were through for the day, as was Irwin. Gilford had expressed a shy body language all morning; Monty's constant frown bunched his eyebrows into little blond caterpillars, and the sun and the wind poufed his blond hair toward Scottish Afro. After kisses on the green from Sally Irwin and Peni Wadkins,

5 Perhaps Hale was just having fun, because he'd done the same thing on the first tee at Royal Lytham in '77, Lanny's Ryder Cup debut. "The north wind was into us and from the left, and it's fifty-two degrees, and Hale says, 'You've gotta hit first here, rook.' I'm like, 'What?' "

Lanny rushed off to grab a sandwich in the trailer. He'd be in battle again in the afternoon, this time with O'Meara.

Stewart/Calcavecchia vs. Woosnam/Faldo

Gallacher said he "could not imagine why" Stockton played Calcavecchia in foursomes. His scouting report said the big boy from Nebraska was too volatile for a format that favored Steady Eddies like Faldo and Woosnam. But there was Calc hitting back-to-back brilliant iron shots on thirteen and fourteen to put the U.S. side two-up. On sixteen, an eight-hundred-yard par five—or did it only seem like half a mile?—*Post and Courier* reporter Forrest White observed an interesting tableau.

"We've still got a chance," said a man standing behind Sheryl Calcavecchia. "Unfortunately, Calcavecchia is putting." When Mark made the six-foot par putt to halve the hole, Sheryl turned to face the doubter and jumped up and down like a cheerleader after a touchdown. On to seventeen, the hardest hole in the world, where about five thousand spectators clustered in the sand amphitheater around the inconvenient green. Payne hit a three iron into the reeds rooted in the pond; then, from the drop zone, a shot of about 120 yards, Mark hit his ball on top of Payne's. Proving Gallacher's point, Calc followed that horrendous stroke with a cannon shot of a tee ball on eighteen.

From the fairway, gum-chewing Payne got an eight iron onto the green. Nick missed; Mark caressed his slightly shorter putt to an impossible-to-miss-from length. After the handshake the losing side brushed past the media and sat in a cart driven by Gallacher. Faldo put his chin in his hand as the train left the station; he and Woosnam had only lost once in eight previous matches and never before this in foursomes. The number one and number two players in the world muttered about their putters. Stewart, the recent U.S. Open champion, retired for an afternoon of lunch, a long session on the practice tee, and spectating. Stockton believed more strongly in the supposedly volatile '89 Open champion and put him out again, with Pavin. Surely, Nick and Ian would avenge themselves in the afternoon against Couples and Floyd.

11

FRIDAY AFTERNOON, SEPTEMBER 27

The crowd had arrived en masse for the first shots of the day. Salt air and exercise sharpened its appetite. It had a drink with lunch; Scott Skornschek of Regency Productions by Hyatt, the official food service company of the '91 Ryder Cup, reported that the $2.50 beer was outselling every other beverage. Worn out from the exertion and seduced by the cool interiors of tents, and by comfortable chairs, TVs, and easy access to food and drink, a significant number said to hell with it. Hard to know by how much, but the afternoon gallery was notably thinner than the enthusiastic horde that had gathered for the first four matches.

Partisans with flags in their hands or poked into their hats had run from shot to shot in the morning, scrambling up dunes and down them, a wearying, sweaty, and BO-producing strategy. Yet this would be the sweetest-smelling gallery in the history of big-time golf, because many years before some coastal Carolinian had discovered that an Avon bath oil called

Skin So Soft discouraged the bites of the scourge of the beach. *Talitridae* were tiny, blood-sucking crustaceans known as sand fleas, beach fleas, sand flies, and no-see-ums. Skin So Soft repelled gnats, too, up to a point, and became a staple of golf shops in coastal Carolina. The whiter the skin, the thinner the skin, so lots of fair-haired fans shelled out eight dollars for a bottle of the heavily perfumed oil.

"I was there, but I don't remember much, because it was so hard to see anything," recalls Sam Nicholson, a lawyer from Augusta, a typical reminiscence from those who attended World War Tee. Galleries rarely have had to work so hard to see so little. Elevated fairways provided magnificent vistas of ocean and beach for the golfers, but left spectators rather sunken. Sand hills often offered the only effective vantage points, and if other aficionados beat you to the best hilltop perches, you just hoped to find an adjacent dune to stand on for the next shot. And the Ocean's astonishing length and unique configuration guaranteed a very long hike. "It's the toughest flat course I've walked," commented Faldo. "We're probably walking ten thousand yards, a third of it through sand." If, as Nick said, the golfers had to walk about 5.68 miles to cover the distance, spectators walked at least a mile or two more, especially if you include the little stroll between the ninth green and the tenth tee.

And then there was that stuff they were walking in. Not for nothing did boxers often run on beaches before the big fight, because the yielding surface made a one-mile jog feel twice that long. The elevation changes of dune walking wearied the legs further, and focused the inevitable competition among thousands of spectators following only four matches.

"This feels too much like work," muttered one out-of shape spectator. "Dreadful," said a photographer from London. "I've never worked on anything like it before, and I hope I never do again. It's very dramatic and you get some great pictures, but it's just too physically demanding."

But seldom were heard such discouraging words, for the excitement of the grand event carried tired legs along. Gaggles of green-armbanded media marched with the players and caddies, a far bigger group than anyone had ever seen before. Usually writers witness a tournament from the press tent and the interview room. "Radio coverage [of a golf tournament] is unheard of in England," said Julian Tutt of the BBC, but there were Tutt and Alan Green and George Bayley murmuring into radio microphones for the bloke in Manchester who couldn't get to a telly. Rocco Mediate, the hyper PGA Tour player from western Pennsylvania, finagled a photographer's assistant gig so he could watch it all from up close. Braswell of *The Post and Courier* recalls seeing a fan inside the ropes trying to blend in with his improvised media credential: a green dish towel knotted around his arm.

"It was much, much more boisterous than a typical golf tournament," recalls Braswell. "The people draped in flags, the organized cheering. I was not expecting anything like that."

Fans grabbed a slice with pepperoni and a Bud and race-walked to the first tee. The format would be fourball: two vs. two, still match play, but everyone plays his own ball and the best score wins. The first match of the afternoon session was bound to be good: The Virginia gunslinger would be facing off against America's favorite Euro, a hairy man who liked to take his shirt off.

•

Americans saw him about as often as they saw the queen of England. Weird that a golfer so good rarely played in North America, but Sam Torrance wedded himself to the Volvo European PGA Tour, playing 685 events on the VEPGAT between '71 and '03, the most ever. After a competition he enjoyed returning to Largs, his seaside hometown on the Firth of Clyde on the west coast of Scotland. During a competition he did not mope in a hotel and order room service. Quite the contrary: As Sam wrote in one of his two autobiographies, après-golf, he and his mates "met in the pub or at a restaurant, not at adjacent exercise bikes or running machines." Torrance liked to toast the end of the day; he did not like to work out or practice. And he liked his Ryder Cup partner, this intense little man from Northern Ireland, and brought him along for the ride.

Match number five. "Teeing off for the European team are Sam Torrance and David Feherty against the team from the United States, Lanny Wadkins and Mark O'Meara."

The light applause died and the actors took deep breaths. The raised, sinuous fairway gave the impression of a very large sleeping snake. The serpent's green back fell off abruptly on both sides, into bright white sand and fifty kinds of tropical foliage, and the palm fronds and spartina and sea oats tangoed in the breeze. Spectators hovered expectantly. All was brightly lit, as if by stage lights. Peter Jacobsen adjusted the weight of his battery pack and audio gear; he would be following this match for TV. Torrance hit first.

A golfer's life turns on the smallest things: a cut or a putt made or missed, a ball bouncing off a tree into the fairway or behind another tree. Torrance's match-point moment occurred during his warm-up tournament the week before the 1983 Ryder Cup in Florida. Sam had arrived in great form; at the end of play in the Southern Open at Green Island Country Club in Columbus, Georgia, he'd tied for first with a journeyman American pro named Ronnie Black. Ronnie plugged his second shot in a bunker on the first hole of the play-off, hacked it out to twenty-five feet, then changed the course of Torrance history by making the putt for a tie. On the fourth hole of sudden death, Black won the play-off, the tournament, the forty-five thousand dollars, and a three-year exemption on the PGA Tour. Torrance was stuck with twenty-seven thousand dollars and a what-if feeling. If he'd won, he'd have moved to the United States. His volubility and humor and amusing accent would have eventually landed him a TV job. He'd have been ubiquitous on the little screen and as a pitchman and as an after-dinner speaker. He'd have become the man and the brand we now know as "Feherty."

The actual Feherty in his first ever Ryder Cup match was so nervous he could hardly stand, barely breathe. The hush of the thousands around the tee and fairway polished an atmosphere already thick with tension. The intense Gallacher and even intenser Seve smoldered on the tee at the start of the afternoon's first game, with Europe severely down in the Match, while the cocksure Lanny Wadkins, the alpha opponent, walked around like he owned the place. David, then thin and clean-shaven, struck his first shots as a Ryder Cupper on autopilot; at least he got his ball onto the green in the regulation two, twenty-five or so feet from the jar.

But then he hit one of golf's most embarrassing shots, the fat putt. Putter scuffed turf before ball; ball rolled like a deflated balloon, four feet wide and six feet short. On the second tee, Torrance put his arm around the shoulders of the younger man. Feherty watched the lips beneath the mustache move. It was a tender moment. "If you don't pull yourself together," said Sam, "I'm going to join them, and you can play all three of us. You useless bastard."

Like Faldo, Torrance had been an only child who grew up in a council house. As Langer's father had, Bob Torrance laid bricks for a living, until he became the greenkeeper and then the pro at the local nine-holer, Routenburn. As with Woosnam, snooker owned his boyish heart almost as much as golf did. And like his mates on this Ryder Cup team, young Sam just couldn't abide school when there was so much else to do. He had joined the workforce at age thirteen, stocking shelves in a grocery store. Later he drove an open-sided, bald-tired whisky truck for an entrepreneur named Jimmy Wham. Dad gave him a good grip and a big shoulder turn and told him the accuracy would come, which it did. His father got him a proper job, too, by calling friends at Sunningdale, the posh club in suburban London. David and Mum flew down for the interview, the first time for either of them on a plane. At lunch, both struggled with the smoked salmon. Do you use a fork or a spoon or pick the damn thing up with your hands?

Smoked: That's what Sam 'n' David were on the front nine. Despite his partner's inspirational speech—and possibly reacting to his putt way short on the first hole—Feherty raced his birdie try on the second green about ten feet past. Unable to make the comebacker, Wadkins and the smooth-swinging O'Meara won the hole with a par five. The Ocean Course greens undulated like a Lebanese belly dancer, and they were fast and getting faster in the constant sunshine and drying wind. Add a bit of nerves to that and . . . Feherty three-putted again on the fifth. He was number one in putting on the Volvo European PGA Tour but you wouldn't know it from these tremulous efforts. Torrance, thirty-eight and in his sixth Ryder Cup, delivered another speech to David, thirty-three, and in his debut. "Try to enjoy this experience," said Sam. "Don't fear it. For how many golfers get to play in the greatest of all tournaments, the Ryder Cup? You Irish arsehole."

They hired Sam at Sunningdale as low man on the assistant pro totem pole for five pounds a week. It was 1970. He was seventeen. His happy-to-be-here attitude charmed the members and his impressive, aggressive play in the regular money matches gained their respect and, when the time came—it came very soon—financial backing for a run as a touring pro.

But the best snapshot of the teenaged Sam may be the one of him at the taping of *Top of the Pops*. Someone from the club gave him a ticket to attend the young people's dance and music TV show, so he rode the thirty miles into London on his heavily mirrored motorbike. Sam would cringe later to recall what a camera hog he'd been, referring to himself as "this gallus[1] hunk of Ayrshire bacon with the dodgy hair." He even volunteered to be part of the background group pretending to be enchanted by every note sung during the solo by Perry Como, who was one of the guest stars that day.

During the practice rounds at Kiawah, Torrance had endeared himself to the fans by walking to the ropes to sign anything they wanted, and by being personable about it, not put off. He also sweated like a sumo in a sauna and smoked at least one fag per hole. His shirttail fell out of the back of his pants. People could *feel* him. Anyone who knew him knew Sam Torrance was a crier. He wept tears of joy when he won the Zambia Open in '75 and when his beloved Danielle or his kids said something touching. The floodgates really opened, of course, on the broad green by the cold pond in front of the clubhouse at the Belfry, the day he holed the putt that at long last won a Ryder Cup for Europe.

Torrance, Feherty, and another fun-loving Irish pro named John O'Leary called themselves "brothers in arms." The brothers eased the dislocated feeling of constant travel and uncertain paydays with glasses of Guinness or Bushmills or what have you. They stayed in bed-and-breakfasts when possible instead of hotels; private homes felt more like home, and the parties were better. In moments of great happiness—a tournament or Ryder Cup win, for example—Sam often adjusted to the warm feeling in the bar by removing his shirt and waving

1 Scottish dialect meaning daring, cheeky, wild; as in "fit for the gallows."

it over his head while leading fellow revelers in song. In 1985 in a pub called the George and Dragon, Tom Kite walked in on this exact scenario—and walked quickly out, as if he'd seen some unholy thing. But it was only the back hair on the chubby Torrance torso. Sam hadn't won anything—this was just a pep rally before the '85 Ryder Cup. "We're gonna beat the Yanks! We're gonna beat the Yanks! Ee aye addio! We're gonna beat the Yanks!"

Feherty hit a wonderful pitch on the par-five seventh for a conceded birdie; O'Meara holed from eight feet to tie. But on the par-three eighth, David left a big C-shaped putt from thirty feet scandalously short. His fourth three-putt left the side two down to cocky Wadkins and impassive O'Meara. Mark O. hit two nearly perfect shots onto the ninth green and a perfect putt from eighteen feet, earning an emphatic high five from Wadkins and then a little neck massage as they walked off the green. Team U.S. had moved to three-up. But on arrival at ten, Feherty seemed to have become a better player. Perhaps the three-quarter-mile road trip had soothed him, given him time to think. Or, as he put it, "I forced my gonads out of my throat." [2] After a too-aggressive third shot to the par-five eleventh, he pitched the ball in from about thirty feet for a winning birdie. His reaction: none.

The fourteenth resembled one of those golfer's nightmare

2 *David Feherty's Totally Subjective History of the Ryder Cup: A Hardly Definitive, Completely Cockeyed, But Absolutely Loving Tribute to Golf's Most Exciting Event,* by James A. Frank and Feherty (New York: Rugged Land, 2004).

holes painted by Loyal H. Chapman—greens on tiny outcroppings by Niagara Falls, tees on top of Mount Everest, forced carries over rooftops on Fifth Avenue in Manhattan, and so on. Fourteen at the Ocean required an almost bizarrely difficult shot of about two hundred yards from the top of one giant sand dune to the top of another. It seemed a mystical place, too, up on that tee, with its view of the sun casting its dying rays on the vast mirror of the Atlantic. Fourteen marks the turn for home, the beginning of the end of a round at the Ocean. And on this day, after nine holes of right-to-left wind, now the breeze pushed balls right, toward the beach. The tide had rolled out.

Feherty hit a thrilling shot, a wind-cutter to about eight feet past the hole. No one else came close. He made the putt. Again, he showed no emotion of any kind. Sam 'n' David were one down now, with four to play.

If Torrance has a dark side, it is well disguised (except, perhaps, for his sleepwalking and anchoring his long putter against his chin). Not so Feherty. Golf and drink and laughing it up with Sam and friends soothed a brilliant mind at war with itself. He held court, the king of jesters; he was a brilliantly funny drunk. The buzz wore off and depression moved in like a thief, making Feherty feel worthless, a fraud. The Bushmills made the depression worse, of course. Heavy dosing of hydrocodone, a painkiller, got him through the day until—an ironic name in this case—Happy Hour. Insomnia required more medication. His undiagnosed attention deficit disorder turned his mind, he said, into a café with fifty-seven voices chattering at once.

Golf provided a bit of refuge, but it also supplied a pretext for excess. For example: After winning the 1986 Scottish Open at Haggs Castle in Glasgow, David smiled for the cameras and held the oldest trophy in sports over his head. That night the party went on a bit. The manager of Led Zeppelin became involved. The new champion regained consciousness two days later, on the sixteenth tee of one of the courses at Gleneagles, an hour's drive from Haggs Castle. The antique silver cup was never seen again.

The Open Championship was Feherty's white whale. Like nearly every golfer not from the United States, it was the tournament he wanted most to win. But the pressure always grew intolerable.

His best chance had been at Royal Troon in '89, the year Calcavecchia won. David had bumped and run his ball around the baked-out course in 71-67-69, three behind the lead held by Wayne Grady. After his round he looked up at the giant main scoreboard, black names and numbers against a field of yellow, and saw his name: FARTERY. "Yeah, right, there's your Open champion," David said, finding self-defeating significance—and an after-dinner anecdote—in a simple misspelling. Feeling himself close to the lead in the eleventh hour of a subsequent Open, he heard an evil voice in his brain whisper, "Better miss this one," and he did.

The light had begun to die when the match came to the seventeenth. Torrance brought the sitting portion of the gallery to its feet with a brilliant shot to two feet. Lanny and O'Meara kept them standing with four-iron shots almost as good, and birdie deuces halved the hole, the only time that would happen the whole weekend. Dormie one for the Americans.

USA Network cut to a blimp shot of the eighteenth green, an emerald amoeba shape on a bed of white. Torrance, Lanny, and O'Meara hit crap second shots into the sand, and Feherty's wasn't much better. At this moment Jacobsen tried something highly unusual and probably ill-advised: an interview with a player during the heat of battle.

Jacobsen, whispering: How good is Sam out of these traps?
Feherty: I can't remember.

Torrance's long try at a four never had a chance. O'Meara fell to the ground after his seemingly perfect putt for par just missed. From about twelve feet, uphill, for the win, Lanny left the infuriating little ball a half an inch short. He leaned his head back and closed his eyes, muttering and motionless. Now Sam 'n' David went around and around, surveying the ground. Feherty's downhill ten-footer to win the hole and tie the match broke a bit left. Or was it right? The inseparable friends disagreed. Bollocks. Which of Feherty's fifty-seven voices or million mischievous cerebral robots or suspect guardian angels would hit this putt?

The ball rolled into the dead center at perfect speed. Finally Feherty showed some emotion. He threw a right uppercut, shook the requisite hands, hugged Torrance, and then he looked ready to weep.

Friday Afternoon Results: Europe 2½, USA 1½

James/Richardson vs. Pavin/Calcavecchia

Pavin hit his first ball as a Ryder Cupper in a camo hat. No one made a big deal of it. The big deal was Big Steve. Stone-faced Mark James got Team Europe two-up with birdies on the second and third, then the large lad from Windsor (the town with the castle) assumed his unique position over a twenty-foot putt for birdie on the sixth: body very low and tilted back, stance so open he almost straddled the line of the putt, and both index fingers extended down the grip. Made it. And Richardson extended his arms with tremendous force on full swings. Over the 537-yard seventh in two, he holed from the sand for eagle three. Three up. He covered all of the 586-yard twelfth with a driver and a long iron, and just missed the eagle putt from four yards. Four up. The Richardson contingent applauded: mum, dad, three sisters, and girlfriend Helen. Dad was the pro at Lee-on-the-Solent Golf Club, a half mile from the Richardson home, a tree-lined acreage Steven had walked innumerable times since he'd picked up a golf stick at age seven. Lee-on-the-Solent was tighter than the Ocean, but with little sand and no crowds, never much at stake, and no ocean. But Richardson swung out like he was back home playing with his mates.

(Courtesy of Kiawah Island Golf Resort)

Pete Dye observed the architecture of Old Scotland and amplified it. A master of camouflage and deception, Dye was as much a part of the '91 Ryder Cup as the players.

(Courtesy of Kiawah Island Golf Resort)

Architect Dye, post-Hugo, hits a six iron on the par-three eighth hole at the Ocean Course. Watching was U.S. Ryder Cup Captain Dave Stockton, who was seeing the course for the first time.

There were twenty-three Ryder Cup players in uniform—and Payne Stewart. Although he lost his singles match to David Feherty, Stewart's sportsmanship and enthusiasm never dimmed.

In an atmosphere between a war-bond rally and the Super Bowl, the wife of an American player makes like Joan of Arc.

Arguably the greatest Ryder Cup team ever. Olazábal suggests a line to Ballesteros.

Seve on safari. Despite occasional wildness off the tee, the Spanish star had a sensational Ryder Cup.

Olazábal and Ballesteros watch Azinger tee off on ten following their protracted argument in the very first match. The Americans "won" the debate—notice Olly's body language.

Fred Couples had had a disastrous Ryder Cup debut in '89 but redeemed himself at the Ocean Course in '91.

Corey Pavin (left) and Captain Stockton celebrate with seawater as the photographer waits to take the team's formal portrait. (See next page.)

Following this stone-dead pitch on sixteen in the final match of the Match, Hale Irwin thought he had clinched the Cup for the United States. He hadn't.

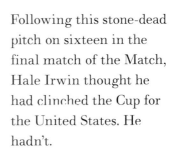

Feherty was beyond thrilled at making a twelve-foot putt to enable a tie for himself and Torrance with Wadkins and O'Meara in a fourball match on Friday afternoon. "Nothing had ever felt like the elation I experienced when that ball went into the hole or the horror at the thought of missing it," he wrote.

Paul Azinger begs his ball to stop somewhere near the hole.

The victorious Americans

The eighteenth green, from the left side of the fairway. Dye recreated the handmade look of Prestwick, the Old Course, Carnoustie, and other ancient Scottish links.

(Courtesy of Kiawah Island Golf Resort)

Splendor in the sea grass. The little figure on the top of the Ryder Cup is modeled after Sam Ryder's instructor, Abe Mitchell.

Couples/Floyd vs. Faldo/Woosnam

"I think the Couples/Floyd team is magic," the analyst in the booth told the afternoon television audience as the four eminences marched down the first fairway. Maybe: With Ray out of the hole, Fred chipped in, Ian and Nick missed birdie putts, and the U.S. side had turned a possible loss into a definite win. But this match hinged far less on the possible supernatural Fred 'n' Floyd pairing and far more on the plain, ugly fact that neither Faldo nor Woosnam could make a putt. Their rising level of discouragement became apparent when Ian did roll one in for birdie at the fourth.

Where was the high five or pat on the back from his partner? Nick just walked to the next tee; exuberance did not fit his style. When they shook hands on the fifteenth green, Floyd beamed. He looked ready to fight a few more rounds. He had finally beaten Faldo in something.

Feherty/Torrance vs. Wadkins/O'Meara

Ballesteros/Olazábal vs. Azinger/Beck

Same winners, same score as in the morning, but a different vibe ruled in the match. Azinger focused fully on his own game and not at all on Seve's. His sensational round included eight birdies and was the best individual performance of the first day. But Chip couldn't buy a putt; perhaps it was unrelated to their relative success with the short stick, but the two Americans spoke less and less as the afternoon wore on. After his artistic birdies on the seventh and eighth holes, the camera pulled in tight on Seve. Ben Wright, imported from CBS TV by USA Network, observed his "lived-in look." And when Azinger complained about leg cramps fifteen thousand yards into his twenty-thousand-yard walk, you had to wonder how Ray Floyd was holding up.

Seve's birdie on the fourteenth put Europe one-up. After Azinger made a birdie putt on sixteen to halve the hole, the Cheer erupted in earnest for the first time: U-S-A! U-S-A! "When I made that putt, I took my hat off," Paul said a few minutes later. "I'm just proud to be an American. . . . And that's what the Ryder Cup is all about."

Debatable; perhaps hitting the green on seventeen was what the Ryder Cup was all about. The man from Pedreña found the seemingly impossible target, but both Azinger and Beck splashed tee balls into the big, bottle-shaped lagoon. Seve could have three-putted and still won the hole and the match, so the Americans had to take off their hats and extend their hands. This win amounted to a crescendo for Team Europe, psychological money in the bank. As he had done all day following holes won, a man from Barcelona waved a big Spanish flag.

End of Day One Score: USA 4½, Europe 3½

Sean Connery and President Bush snapped off their televisions. Television producer Larry Cirillo of NBC, and Captains Stockton and Gallacher each gathered with coworkers for dinner in their snug quarters at Kiawah. Buses rumbled off the island. A select few clattered off in Bell Jet Rangers for a twilight helicopter ride back to their cars at Brittlebank Park, Wild Dunes up on Isle of Palms, or, for those who could only stay the day, to their little jets at Charleston Executive Airport on Johns Island. Restaurants filled up. Tiffany Hills stepped into the spotlight in the Crazy Horse Revue. An unseen hand cranked up Willie Tee and the Magnificents performing "Little John" and the clubgoers began to shag, shag, shag!

And the sunburned veterans of the Battle of the Coast analyzed the day. Think we'll see Steve Pate tomorrow? they asked. Think we'll see Dan Quayle?

PART FOUR
MADE FOR TV

Perfection, so attractive in the abstract, when sought in reality just places her hands on her slim hips and laughs elusively.

—*Neil Steinberg,* Complete and Utter Failure

12

RATINGS RACE

Like most major sporting events of the last half century, the 1991 Ryder Cup was at heart a television show. Only a tiny fraction of the Ryder Cup audience walked the sandy ground with the participants in the drama; the Battle of the Coast played out primarily in living rooms and nineteenth holes and above the bartender's head.

In a by-then familiar arrangement, a cable provider—in this case, USA Network—teamed with an over-the-air network—NBC—to cover the big event. NBC would have the prime time on Saturday afternoon and the singles matches on Sunday, while USA Network would man the helm for all of Friday and the first half of Saturday. "It was our engineers and equipment, and a combination of our and their announcers," says NBC's producer, Larry Cirillo. "They paid us a fee—fifty thousand dollars or whatever." The revenue from commercials went to the entity broadcasting them. While others in the cable/satellite business lived on subscriber fees—HBO and Showtime, for example—USA Network made money by punctuating its Ryder Cup broadcast with spots from Shearson Lehman, Wendy's, Metropolitan Life Insurance, Karsten Manufacturing (Ping golf clubs), Subaru, and Mitsubishi electronics. It aired a bit of self-promotion, too, such as a trailer for its own movie, *White Lie*, starring tap-dancer-turned-actor Gregory Hines, whose character is on a quest to find the man who killed his daddy.

Since its start as the Madison Square Garden Network in 1971, USA had filled much of its programming holes with sports. Complementing rerun cartoons, movies, and game shows were the Westminster Kennel Club's annual dog competition, early rounds of U.S. Open tennis, and, since 1982, the first two rounds of the Masters. It had paid $200,000 to broadcast eight and a half hours of the '89 Ryder Cup, but none of the big three piggybacked on the deal that year.

Why didn't ABC, CBS, or NBC step up? Ratings. Even as it ascended as a competitive event worthy of attention, the Ryder Cup had not been a particularly valuable television property, in part because it took place after the summer golf season and during the American football season. ABC had broadcast two and a half hours of the Cup in '79, '83, and '85, achieving Nielsen ratings just above or below 2.[1] But the golfers in the boardroom at 30 Rockefeller Center perceived a Halley's Comet

1 A rating gives the estimated percentage of TVs tuned in to a specific program. If the United States had a hundred million households with televisions in 1991, one point would equal one million watchers. But since the system is based on a sample balanced between urban and rural, rich and poor, and black, white, and Pacific Islander, nineteenth holes and sports bars were sure to be underrepresented.

of potential and voted to buy the rights for '91 for just under $2 million. "NBC would be thrilled (and lucky) to get a modest 3," wrote Richard Sandomir in *The New York Times.*

Sandomir's skepticism that the Cup could draw a large audience was well founded. The competition for viewers, he knew, would be fierce. On Saturday, for example, CBS would broadcast the Minnesota Twins and the Blue Jays of Toronto, one of Major League Baseball's final regular-season games. ABC had Florida State at Michigan from two to six P.M., an interregional game between college football powerhouses guaranteed to attract a large TV audience. ESPN countered with more football—Auburn at Tennessee, then Southern Cal at Oregon. Mississippi State/Florida was on TBS. And that was just the Saturday competition. Pro football ruled on Sunday. Fortunately for NBC, it had the big game—the Dolphins at the Jets—and kickoff wasn't scheduled until four P.M. The Ryder Cup would be its lead-in.

Pressure descended on the TV people for some of the same reasons it sat on the shoulders of the golfers. The Friday eight-A.M.-to-five-P.M. show would be the longest continuous live golf telecast in TV history. The planned total broadcast time for the three days would be twenty-one and a half hours, an exhausting, exhilarating ordeal for cast and crew (the actual time on the air would be twenty-four hours).

"Long days," recalls Cirillo. "No carousing, that's for sure. We'd have an early dinner and go to bed. You had to edit yourself the way you edited a piece of tape. But we got caught up in the excitement, just like the players, and we ran on adrenaline. . . . I've done all kinds of events, including the

Olympics and the Super Bowl, but the emotions of that Ryder Cup, especially on the last day, were unlike anything I ever saw."

NBC golf was known for its work in less exalted venues. The PGA Tour in winter groaned under the weight of low-prestige tournaments with celebrity first names, and the Peacock Network covered them. Cirillo shepherded twenty-one years of the Bob Hope Chrysler Classic, twelve iterations of the Dinah Shore, and eighteen of the Andy Williams San Diego Open, and got to know Bob, Dinah, and Andy along the way, but he longed for bigger game. For years Cirillo had lobbied his bosses for a grander stage. Why can't we get the U.S. Open? Meanwhile, his friendly rival Frank Chirkinian of CBS put another feather in his and his network's hat with each annual broadcast of the Masters. But with this Ryder Cup, Cirillo finally had a worthy platform, free of the enervating fluff inherent in having becardiganed Jay Randolph ask suntanned Andy what he thought of this year's tournament and, by the way, tell us about your charity. He'd broadcast enough episodes of Bob Hope posing with seven busty babes whose tight white T-shirts spelled out his name, one letter per chest.

The heat was on USA and NBC's golf teams like it had never been before. Would everyone involved in the production of the War by the Shore rise to the occasion?

No. But it would put us close enough to the players to see the terror crossing their eyes, and to set a tone that future Cup broadcasts would emulate. They managed what every live TV show aspires to: a sense of drama and of history being made.

The epic broadcast opened with a dreamy shot of morning

sunshine on the sea. "Less than an hour after sunrise," began Bill Macatee. "A barrier island in South Carolina called Kiawah greets a new day. The timeless rhythm of the Atlantic; the serenity of the marshes and the dunes; all provide a unique setting for an event that in many ways reminds us of why we fell in love with sports to begin with. . . ."

While the foot soldiers with battery packs and microphones provided snippets of information—and a couple of them, Bob Trumpy and Peter Jacobsen, delivered especially graceful telegrams from the front—the show would swim or sink based on the performance of the three men in the booth. Moderator Macatee, at age thirty-five already a veteran of nine years as an NBC sportscaster, smoothly did what he was supposed to do, which was to set up the other guys. On his left sat Bentley (Ben) Wright, a resident of North Carolina but an Englishman by birth, whose accent and background covering golf for the *Financial Times* of London made him in theory the expert regarding Team Europe. But he was hardly in anyone's pocket, and in fact had infuriated Captain Gallacher with something he had written before the match, and during it by saying that the Euros did not have the look of a team pulling together.

The erudite Wright had debuted with CBS in 1972, as a man on a TV tower at the Masters, where he was proud to be the protégé of droll Henry Longhurst, also a Brit and a newspaperman moonlighting on TV. "We are caption writers in a visual medium," Henry told the younger man one day over a glass of gin; good advice that stuck.

On Macatee's right waited a little ball of tension named Peter Kostis, a golf instructor, often of Tour pros, including Calcavecchia. A Mainer, Kostis had played a bit of football at the University of New Hampshire before turning his focus to fixing backswings and grips. His career as a TV broadcaster had started precisely two years earlier, at the Ryder Cup in England in '89, when someone from USA Network discovered that Peter would be at the Belfry giving lessons, and recruited him to go on the air and say something.

Wright was a journalist, with a witty delivery—you knew he knew this wasn't really a war—and had a journalist's instinct to report what he saw. Not so the keyed-up Kostis, whose malapropisms and know-it-allism undermined his own insight and the efforts of the other performers. He observed the obvious: "That putt is short and to the right." When the other announcers made a point, he corrected it or attempted to improve it. "Visually, can he see the pin?" he asked. "It's not that he's been scared," he said of O'Meara, "but he's been that kind of afraid."

What? It might have been interesting to hear the conversation as Azinger and his caddie debated strategy and club selection on an iron shot to the sixteenth green, but Kostis would not let the pictures and the players tell the story.

When Macatee and Wright shared an anecdote about Couples's sad meltdown on the final hole of his final match in the previous Ryder Cup—this was brought up in the context of how well he was playing at Kiawah—Kostis responded mystifyingly. "Well, I don't believe any of it," he said. "I know it happened."

Huh? Apparently, Peter could not countenance the idea that his friend Fred had fallen apart in a crisis. And when the instructor/announcer addressed his preshot comments to the player hitting them—"just go through your process, have faith in your swing"—his master weakness as an announcer was laid bare. He thought more about the players than he did about the viewers. He liked the players. They employed him. He was an insider loyal to the inside.

But others appreciated Kostis's willingness to intrude himself into the event, understanding that he was not built to be an arm's-length observer. "It's not difficult to see why so many PGA Tour players seek out Peter Kostis," wrote the estimable Larry Dorman in *Golf World* in a review of the TV coverage. "The man has an impeccable eye and a succinct delivery. He knows the players and does the best swing analysis on television, bar none."

At two o'clock on Saturday afternoon, the USA crew passed the baton, and as NBC signed on, a new group took over the booth. The network's analyst, who had the authority of having played in Ryder Cups and won majors, would root, root, root for the home team, which was annoying for anyone who might have been expecting an even hand. He might have been partisan, but Johnny Miller did not mince words.

13

SATURDAY, SEPTEMBER 28

Weary from two nights of being wakened every three hours for electrotherapy on his sore side, Pate had wandered about on Thursday and Friday, inventing new ways to answer the question people kept asking him. More than once he lifted his shirt for curious friends, like LBJ showing off his appendectomy scar. Underneath an Ace bandage, the big blue bruise above Pate's left hip and lower back covered an area the size of two hands. By Sunday it would have progressed all the way through the rainbow to finish at mottled black. "If this Ryder Cup thing doesn't work out, I have a tremendous future as a crash test dummy," he joked. And: "Playing bumper cars in limos isn't a real good idea."

NBC found him on Friday afternoon in the Pavin/Calcavecchia gallery, his face shaded by the same kind of homely camo cap Corey was wearing. Steve had hit about a hundred balls that morning, but he couldn't swing very hard, maxing out at about three-quarter speed. "It's the first time I've galleried a tournament in six years," he said. "It's killin' me."

And it was killing Stockton. "I had two set pairings going in," Captain Dave would recall. "Actually three; my strongest team was going to be Pavin and Pate. Being from USC and picking two UCLA Bruins to go together, it would have been magical. Pate never shot above sixty-seven in practice—playing phenomenal. I hadn't put Pavin with anybody else in practice and I had to jockey him around, which I knew cost us points."

But after the sixteen Saturday-morning players warmed up and went off to battle, Pate appeared on the practice tee with his caddie and his clubs. He was going to give it a try in the afternoon fourball match, teaming up at last with his friend and fellow limo-crash survivor Pavin. While Steve took experimental swings and waited for the Advil to kick in, matches nine through twelve made their tortuous way around the Ocean Course. On another brightly lit day by Kiawah's broad beach, the wind blew again from the land toward the sea. A cool breeze; both teams wore white sweaters for the first hour or two. Blue slacks and pinkish shirts for the Euros, khaki-color pants and red shirts for the Yanks.

In this corner, in the day's first match, Gallacher was giving Sam 'n' David another chance after their slightly miraculous tie of the previous afternoon; they'd be playing—oh, dear—speed-walking Wadkins and intimidating Irwin. The final morning contest looked like a title bout, with the undefeated Seve 'n' Olly against the equally undefeated Freddie 'n' Floyd. Match three held great interest, too, because it announced the demise of partnerships that had gone sour. Despite Paul's extraordinary play, Azinger/Beck had lost twice on Friday. Chip would have the day to sit in the corner (actually he walked around the course, holding hands with his lovely wife, Karen), while Zinger would try again for his first point with O'Meara. Their opponent would be Nick Faldo and, not Ian Woosnam.

"My banker's pairing," Gallacher had called this previously very successful team. But now the bank was closed, if not insolvent. At Muirfield Village in '87, when the partnership began, it had three wins and a tie. Faldo/Woosnam scorched the earth in their fourth match: ten under par in fourteen holes! (Kite and Strange were the victims.) Two wins and a tie at the Belfry in '89, then on Saturday afternoon a loss that was no disgrace: Azinger/Beck best-balled an incredible thirteen under par to win 2 and 1.

But that was so two years ago. The Nick and Woosie divorce provided fodder for the writers: With Ian the world number one, and Faldo number two, had this become a team of chiefs and no Indians? Some European journos mused about Woosie's humdrum play since winning the Masters and ascending to the top of the rankings. The little Welshman had been vacationing in Barbados as an antidote to the chill winds back home in Wales; perhaps *la dolce vita* had blurred his focus.

But a simpler explanation for the failure of Faldo/Woosnam was that neither man could make a damn putt. From the moment they mispronounced the name of the world's top player on the first tee of his first match—"Ian Woosnin"—Woosie at Kiawah seemed an unfamiliar version of himself. Angry Woosie frequently raised his arms in a despairing gesture, as if dark forces had conspired to make the ball roll off the lip. He stared at the head of his Zebra putter, as if demons were in there. He'd found the lady-size, stripe-headed mallet with a crooked grip at the beginning of the 1990 season, while noodling around in the pro shop of his home course, Oswestry Golf Club in England. It had been the club that got him to the top, but now the love affair lay in tatters. Or three putts. Meanwhile Faldo muttered, "My touch is gone," and admitted to being "terrified" on the greens. "Nick was a bit anti-everything that week," recalls David Leadbetter, his instructor. Among other things, he couldn't get the loft and lie of his putter quite right.

In the Friday-night conference in the captain's suite in Building 500, amid beer-can-covered tables, Faldo, Woosnam, and Langer had complained about what shite they were playing (although Bernhard would never use so vulgar a word). But one of this big three would have to play in the morning; Gallacher decided it would be Nick. Now the question became with whom to pair him: Gilford or Montgomerie? The two rookies had been filleted by Lanny and Hale on Day One. "I didn't know Monty that well," Nick would recall in his aptly named autobiography, *Faldo: In Search of Perfection.* "So I asked who was playing better. David was the reply; he was hitting everything straight down the middle."

And off they went. Gilford studied the second shot from the first fairway for long moments. If books were covers, you'd guess accountant or actuary, and you wouldn't be far off. When the quiet man was not doing battle on the golf course, he communed with his herd of Herefords on fifty acres in north Staffordshire, in central England. The dairyman who had won the English Open struck a strong iron shot but it would not hold, and the ball bounced over the green, into the sand. Faldo had driven too short, so Gilford had had to hit a low lofted club, which came in too hot to stick; their first failure to play nicely with each other.

From a little farther down the fairway Azinger carved a very good shot into the breeze to the tight front right pin, about eighteen feet from the hole. A marshal's hat blew across the fairway and into the water by the fairway; the gallery—perhaps it was keyed up and needed a comic release—applauded. Faldo could not do much with his awkward shot; O'Meara holed for birdie three. And the worst rout in Ryder Cup history[1] had begun.

The second shot to the dogleg left par-four third played dead into the wind, but the ball could not be brought in low because of a handful of intervening trees and because the green sat on a high mesa with abrupt fall-offs on the sides—it looked like the top of a volcano. Gilford hit a good-looking shot over those odd-looking live oaks, whose growth on their beach-side had been retarded by greater exposure to saltwater blown in from the sea. The ball landed well on the surface and within a few yards of the flapping white flag, but it would not rest. The ball paused, uncertain, almost stopped, rolled slowly to the front of the green and then quickly thirty yards down to the base of the hill. From there Nick hit a lovely pitch, but David could not wiggle in the four-footer. Two down. . . . We could go on and on

1 There had been one equally lopsided eighteen-hole team match, when Irwin and Tom Kite beat the bangers and mash out of Ken Brown and Des Smyth by the same score in alt. shot in '79.

like this, but no one hole or shot or gesture can fully illuminate this debacle. It had the drama of a funeral. Gilford looked intimidated by the stage or perhaps a bit unsettled by the silence of his partner. Faldo's preoccupation with his own problems announced his indifference to David's. Azinger had the perfect stinging ball flight to handle the blustery wind; O'Meara was making putts and no mistakes. And the next-to-impossible golf course amplified the discouragement felt by the side behind.

The gale blew Team Europe's blue trousers flat against its legs, limning kneecaps, thighs, and shins. Anatomical outlines didn't show up as well with the Yankees' pleated off-white pants. The temperature ascended to seventy, then to seventy-five, the afternoon high. Lips began to chap, skin began to burn.

On the fifth green Nick stood behind David's putt for a birdie two, but he did so with his arms crossed, and he did not squat to get the worm's-eye view. Gilford missed, Azinger made. One hundred yards away, waves rolled rapidly in and simmered on the sand. Three down. Two holes later, Faldo's body language spoke more clearly. The Euros got their ball to a few yards off the right edge of the green on the par-five seventh, but into a bare lie. Faldo chunked the chip, just hit the turf behind the ball like a hacker, a shocking sight. Zinger had hit a magnificent and slightly lucky two iron onto the surface and fifteen feet from the pin. A conceded eagle; five down. Nick walked toward the next tee with his shoulders slumped, a defeated man. "A spent force," said Wright.

The match ended, the score 7 and 6. Faldo made as if to get the hell out of there—who could blame him?—momentarily forgetting the hat removal and handshake ritual. Caddie Fanny gently shooed him back onto the twelfth green.

With sharp knives, the European press carved up poor Nick for the embarrassing futility of seven and six. Why hadn't he encouraged—or even talked to—his young teammate? Seve would have. Even Torrance found fault with the remote way Faldo had acted. Something Alistair Cooke had written about King Edward VIII came to mind: that he was at his best when the going was good. In his memoir Woosie remembered the Cup of '87, when love was new, and he and Faldo were "encouraging each other, advising each other, and congratulating each other: Nick and I appeared almost unstoppable."

So, big deal: Like most people, Faldo withdrew when fortune seemed to be favoring the other guy. "He is a loner," Captain Gallacher would explain. "Like all Cancerians, he does from time to time disappear into his protective shell, but his only thought [after the match] was to sort out his putting so that he could win a singles point on the last day to avoid the embarrassment of a personal whitewash." Faldo summoned Leadbetter, and together they worked for three hours, including a long period chipping and putting around the first three greens after the afternoon matches had passed through.

McCumber conducted the interview with the winning team. O'Meara observed that Paul's two-iron shot on number seven "stuck the old knife in the coffin"—a novel metaphor. At any rate, Azinger finally had his point, the first in a very good morning for the U.S. team. Each of its pairs won—except the team that until then hadn't lost.

Wadkins/Irwin vs. Feherty/Torrance

One of the media foot soldiers corralled a camera and Bob Torrance and put them together.

Mick Luckhurst: We're with the father of Sam Torrance, who also is the golf instructor for David Feherty and Ian Woosnam. How do you think the match is going? How do you think Sam is doing?

Torrance senior owned a coastal Scotland burr as strong as single malt and a deep-in-his-throat delivery, and the more he spoke, the older the Scotch got. He sounded like an idling Harley. "That might have been easier with subtitles," said Wright, "or an interpreter."

Bob had probably observed that the east wind, steady at fifteen miles per hour but with stronger gusts, was drying out the already dry greens, making the course play even tougher than the day before. The essence of the Ocean was a trip through hell to get to the putting surface, he might have said, and then no reward when you got there. Just more torture of shiny grass on slick slopes.

The match seesawed on the front nine; Irwin/Wadkins took a one-up lead with a birdie on ten. "I thought Feherty and Torrance were a bit resigned to the outcome fairly early in the match," recalls Mike Bylen, a golf course owner from Michigan, and a fierce partisan for Wadkins, his friend since 1976. Bylen always traveled to the Ryder Cup to watch his pal.

"Lanny and Hale were down the middle and on the green, leaving no openings and no easy holes. I think Sam and David knew it."

But they didn't act like they knew it until they lost the final three holes—fourteen, fifteen, and sixteen—alternate-shotting in double bogey, bogey, and let's go have a beer. With this point, the 17½th of his Ryder Cup career, Wadkins had moved to third on the all-time list for Team U.S., past Nicklaus and Trevino, and trailing only Casper (20) and Palmer (22).

During a postmatch TV interview, Lanny recalled his first-ever Ryder Cup competition. It had been a foursomes game against Bernard Gallacher and pipe-smoking Brian Barnes. "My nerves were a lot better in '77, but I had the same partner," Lanny said. "Hale and I, we've done pretty good. We're 3 and 0 as a team. I'll take Hale anytime, believe me."

The Kostis explanation for Lanny's success: "He's one of the few players still on the American Tour who doesn't play practice rounds. Essentially, he'll go out and play a few dollars here and there in Nassau. He loves to have that challenge in front of him."

Translation: Wadkins did, of course, play practice rounds. He bet on them.

Azinger/O'Meara vs. Faldo/Gilford

Calcavecchia/Stewart vs. James/Richardson

As usual, Stewart was the only one of the twenty-four players out of uniform; they let him wear his Sansabelt plus-twos, tam, and kneesocks. He is vivid in memory, as we imagine him hitting a fearless iron shot in waltz tempo to the scary twelfth green, with the white flag right and water right, and in the water, to the delight of TV, the eye ridge and snout of a cruising alligator. Holding his follow-through in brilliant sunshine, Payne's jaws work over a piece of gum as he gazes at the ball hanging in the air; the spheroid hits, and sits, and Stewart waves briefly to acknowledge the applause. Then his slim, fit partner rolls in the eight-footer to put the U.S. side two up. While these four enjoyed a number of similar successes, failure was the brush that painted the portrait of the end of this match.

How Calc despised the final five! The by now chronic left-to-right wind accentuated his fade, leading to swings that were wild or irresolute. From an upslope in the middle of the fifteenth fairway, he pulled a four-iron shot into the gallery in the sand on the left. On the par-five sixteenth, he blew his tee ball into the gallery in the sand to the right. Payne chopped it out; with a driver, Calc hit a majestic, wind-aided slice over the gallery back into the sand fleas and silica on the right, damn near on the beach. "That could be in Bermuda," said Jacobsen.

And then they came to seventeen, the hole Mark and everyone else *really* hated. Payne hated it first, dunking his iron shot from 181 into the lagoon (he'd hit roughly the same shot with the same result the day before). With the wind blowing so hard it made little waves in the pond, Richardson slashed a low hook onto the surface, a wonderful shot to the skinny target. From the drop area—yes, he had done the same thing on Friday—Mark dumped it in the water. Team U.S. held a one-up lead with one to play.

"There are two places that Payne Stewart has never reached," typed Hubert Mizell of the *St. Petersburg Times* that afternoon. "Outer Mongolia and the seventeenth green at the Ocean Course." He could have written the same thing about Calcavecchia.

James, a hooker, blocked his tee ball dead right on eighteen and swore with great feeling. Stewart, from the fairway 190 yards from the green, knocked his iron shot into the desert short and right. After a few more comic misadventures and a very good pitch by James, Richardson had a four-foot putt for a four to win the hole and tie the match. He missed.

Ballesteros/Olazábal vs. Couples/Floyd

The Spaniards were better all day. Seve took aggressive lines to fairways and greens and putted beautifully. Olazábal, yin to Seve's yang, was a diamond cutter, methodical, patient, and very precise. The Yanks birdied only one hole in the match, a two-putt four on the downwind seventh. "We didn't make anything," said Ray in the aftermath, but "they made a lot of putts"—the classic loser's postmortem, but quite true in this case. While on camera, Floyd learned from his interviewer that he was through for the day. Surprise and disappointment flickered across Ray's face, but he quickly recovered and said something about supporting the team. And so the much-praised Floyd/Couples partnership ended with two wins and one loss, a more formidable force in memory than it was in actuality.[2]

Saturday morning had been close to a disaster for Team Europe—pretty much the same deal as Friday morning. It was crazy: Alt. shot was a standard country-club format in Europe but Americans never played it, except in the Ryder Cup. So why were they better at it? No one knew, or even had a good guess.

On the other hand, the Euros owned the Yanks in fourball. In the two vs. two game, polyglot Europe united. Woosnam and others put forth the tosh that the wonderful family feeling on the Continental side explained its fourball success (then why did the family fail in foursomes?). At any rate, from 1985 through the first day at Kiawah, Europe earned twice as many fourball points as the U.S. side. The stat predicted success for Gallacher's boys on Saturday afternoon. And so it came to pass.

Saturday morning results: USA 3, Europe 1
Total score: USA 7½, Europe 4½

2 They would look for the magic one more time, two years later, at the Belfry, and not find it. Fred and Ray would be drubbed 5 and 4 by Faldo and Montgomerie.

14

SATURDAY AFTERNOON, 2:00 P.M. EST

The Executive Branch of the United States of America didn't do it for the World Series or the Super Bowl or even for the Olympics. But as you channel surfed before the Florida State/Michigan game, you saw a still shot of the Presidential Seal, and then President George H. W. Bush, seated, smiling, in a gray suit and muted red tie, opening the NBC telecast of this once humble golf exhibition. He appeared to be in his hotel room in Sea Island, Georgia, where he and Bar were vacationing:

> Good afternoon. It's a pleasure to tee off this biannual golf classic, the world famous Ryder Cup. As every weekend golfer with a hard slice knows, the Ryder Cup brings together the best golfers in the United States and Europe. The battle for the Cup has made this tournament one of golf's most competitive contests. By bringing together nations and people in friendly competition, the Ryder Cup

> reflects the finest tradition in sports. And while only one team can claim victory, I'll show my patriotic colors for a moment by hoping that the American team brings the Cup back here where it belongs, right here in the United States. Thank you, and let the round begin.

That the president of the United States took the time to introduce the broadcast showed not only the extraordinary interest in this edition of the Cup, it also spoke to the importance of golf in the White House. The elder Bush was an active man, almost hyperactive, and he loved golf as long as he could get it over with quickly—a perfect partner for Lanny, Bush played almost at a run. Golf was in his genes. Both his maternal grandfather and his father had been presidents of the USGA. Grandpa George Herbert Walker gave the world the Walker Cup (the amateur version of the Ryder Cup) and bestowed to his grandson his first and two middle names.

And Quayle! The vice president owned the strongest game of any heartbeat-away man in American history. Critics dismissed Dan Quayle as "the Bush Administration's golf pro," a partisan insult disguised as a compliment. A thoroughly smitten golfer, Quayle had played three years for the DePauw Tigers of Greencastle, Indiana, and as a senator from the Hoosier State, DQ had kept his handicap at or near scratch. After getting some heat for taking an air force jet for a fact-finding mission to Augusta National, he played a lot less, but the VP still maintained a six.

In short, the men at the top of the U.S. government knew and loved the greatest game. And on Sunday, the vice president and his wife, Marilyn, would be on the sandy ground at Kiawah, for a bit of spectating and participation in the closing ceremony. And, maybe, some golf. Dan brought his clubs. "This guy doesn't pass a golf course without stopping," one of his sunglassed security detail said.

TV viewers who stayed with NBC after the Bush intro got a three-minute Ryder Cup history lesson—superbly done, narrated by the penetrating baritone of Charlie Jones, and with a tolerable amount of the slow motion, gauze focus, and treacly music endemic to the genre.

> How did it happen that a friendly golf match has come to this? How did the spirit of innocence and fraternity turn to rampant nationalism and frenzy? When did the metaphors begin to sound more like football and boxing? Indeed, did someone so conservative as Jack Nicklaus actually say that this weekend would be a war? When there is more at stake for a professional golfer than merely playing for a sponsor's money, when the stakes are team and country, then maybe Jack Nicklaus is right. Maybe this is a war on Kiawah Island. But not a war that we can see, because the battle in golf is always internal. . . . The struggle to silence one's body and senses, to quiet one's breath, and mind.[1]

The USA Network booth had been manned by a troika, but NBC went into battle armed with just two voices. Jones, sixty, a

1 Jones, Cirillo, and writer/statistician John Goldstein collaborated on the script for the short history of the Cup.

bespectacled, gray-haired gent from Fort Smith, Arkansas, had been with NBC since 1965. His smooth-as-silk tones, darkened by cigarette smoke—you'd like to hear him sing "For the Good Times" or "Ol' Man River"—had been impossible to miss if you watched sports on TV. Jones did football mostly but also called Olympics, World Cup, Wimbledon tennis, and golf. He had a factual yet dramatic style; perhaps his law degree from the University of Arkansas informed what he said and how he said it.

John Laurence Miller sat on his right. *That's* Johnny Miller? We hadn't seen him in a while; his hair looked shorter and less sun-bleached and he'd finally filled out. Following his days of ubiquity in the 1970s, Miller had slowly faded from view. He'd first pricked the national consciousness in 1966, when, as a nineteen-year-old amateur, he'd finished T-8 in the U.S. Open on his home course, the Olympic Club in San Francisco. He turned pro after getting a degree in Phys. Ed from Brigham Young, then dazzled with three bolts of lightning: a final round 63 to win the '73 U.S. Open at Oakmont; eight tournament wins in '74, the most since Arnold Palmer won eight in '62; and the introduction of the Johnny Miller Collection in the late fall of '74. Slender, lank-haired Johnny in plaids and patterns and polyester leisure suits—for the next few years Sears blanketed the Western world with images of its spokesmodel. Miller won another major, the '76 Open Championship; played on Ryder Cup teams in '75 and '81; and then receded into the background. With a growing family, a new house in Napa, a Porsche built for the wine country's curvy roads, and real wealth, conservatively invested, from his endorsements, who needed golf? That the ability to putt very well had left him made the quiet life of part-time competition and golf-course design still more attractive. Then Larry Cirillo came calling.

As December 1, 1989, approached—his fiftieth birthday—and Lee Trevino became eligible for the easy (for him) money on the Senior PGA Tour, everyone involved knew he would quit as NBC's lead golf analyst. Cirillo had an inspiration while producing an NFL game in Denver in December. "I went down to the tournament in Tucson [in January of '90] and met Johnny Miller. I said, 'How would you like to take Lee Trevino's place?' He says, 'Uh, no.' He was so introverted."

But Cirillo was a persuasive man and Miller finally agreed to give announcing a shot at the Bob Hope Desert Classic a month later. Cirillo: "He comes in on Monday. He's got problems [on Wednesday, the first round of the five-round tournament], but he's pretty good. At seven A.M. Thursday I get a call from Charlie Jones. He says, 'Larry, we've got a problem. Johnny was in the hospital last night. He doesn't think he can go today.' I go to meet him at his hotel. He's got the covers up around his neck and a little hat on his head and he's in this Louis XIV bed that must be six feet off the ground. I jump up on the bed. He says, 'I can't talk.' We discuss it for forty minutes. You know what his problem was? Stage fright."

He overcame it. But he did not have to overcome any fear about speaking honestly on the air because he didn't know any other way. The standard-issue golf pro/announcer was a self-censoring compatriot of the players he was allegedly analyzing, but Miller had never been one of the boys on Tour. As a Mormon, he could not, would not, meet a peer for a drink or even for coffee. His wife, Linda, and the kids accompanied him on the Tour, so he had little time or inclination to socialize with the other players. "He certainly wasn't a backslapper," says San Francisco–based attorney Butch Berry, Miller's friend of forty years. "He was and remains supremely confident, but also very self-critical and hard on himself. I think he worked out his anxieties at the wheel of his Porsche." From the Golden Gate Bridge, past Novato and Sonoma, and all around the rounded hills of the vineyards, Johnny drove his German sports cars *very* fast.

"I was the first guy to get real," Miller said once. "The old guard was used to being complimented for the good stuff and ignoring the bad stuff. It's the way I critiqued my own game. If I messed up, I would say so. It's not like I changed when I got into the booth."

Johnny's candor included using the most fraught word in sports: *choke*. No one in the booth at a golf tournament had dared bring up the c-word before. Golfers' eggshell egos rarely allow them to admit what they know to be true, that pressure and stress can trump their concentration and skill. Miller informed the world when he thought a breakdown had been caused by choking—not by a sudden gust of wind, or by a misjudged yardage, or the caddie, or sunspots. His bluntness infuriated the players. After reviewing NBC's coverage on Saturday evening, Azinger would say, "Johnny Miller is the biggest moron who has ever been in the booth." The next day Azinger recovered brilliantly: "There was a misprint in the paper yesterday. The writers left out a letter. I meant biggest *Mormon* in the booth."

Although his approach caused a sensation among viewers, no one could maintain that Miller was flawless, or even as good as

Wright. To the point of meaninglessness, he used *fall line*—a skiing term—as a way to describe the topography of greens. He and Jones were seldom content to let the unadorned pictures tell the story. And Johnny initiated a completely unedifying piece of dialogue with the reporter by the green, a ritual exchange that has not changed in the decades since the '91 Ryder Cup:

Miller: What do you think, Rog? This putt breaks about a ball to the left?

Maltbie: It all depends on how hard he hits it, Johnny.

But when Miller observed the glacial pace of Olazábal preparing to hit a sand shot, a refreshing breath of honesty wafted through the booth: "José María is a very deliberate player. Actually, that's being kind. He's slow."

The NBC telecast on Saturday afternoon had a touch more polish than USA Network had been able to muster. Following the impressive greeting from the president of the United States, and the well-conceived Ryder Cup history lesson, Jones and Miller had a few brief comments regarding the weather and the feeling of Ryder Cup pressure. The foot soldiers checked in. Jacobsen, McCumber, Maltbie, and Mark Rolfing (recovering from using the word *discomboobulate* on the first day of the USA broadcast) were each walking with a match in progress. And the swings and putts and grimaces began.

Europe was down, and desperate. Fatigue had entered the equation; Azinger, Couples, Wadkins and Ballesteros, James, and Olazábal were each attempting their fourth round in two days, a forty-thousand-yard march—nearly twenty-three miles—according to Faldo's calculation. Each side entered the last player on its bench. Both were Ryder Cup rookies: Paul Broadhurst, a twenty-six-year-old Englishman from a little town near Birmingham; and Wayne Levi, thirty-nine, from upstate New York and SUNY Oswego. Couples had a new partner, as did Woosie, Zinger, Langer, and, for the third time in this Match, Lanny.

As the finish line came into view—just this fourball game and Sunday's singles remained—the crowd grew restive. Not louder, until the end of the day, because the home team fell quickly behind. Beer consumption surely increased the partisanship. Greensides echoed with football (soccer) songs. The dumbfounded American portion of the crowd responded with the only arrow in its quiver: U-S-A! U-S-A! U-S-A!

Perhaps the most interest in the Saturday-afternoon matches attached to the wounded warrior, Pate. Would he collapse and leave on a stretcher, or overcome his pain to turn in a performance they'd write songs about? He and Corey walked to the first tee, both wearing those camo hats the Euros hated so much.

"I'll hit first and take the pressure off you," Langer told Montgomerie on the practice tee. Brilliant, replied Monty—clipped English from the German, a pleasant timbre and English accent from the Scot. No doubt about leadership on this team . . . but Bernhard launched the first drive in match fourteen directly and shockingly *recht,* over the crowd and deep into the jungle. Monty managed a little laugh. "Thank you, Bernhard," he said, then hit a conservative shot, with a three wood, 230 yards and into the fairway. Pate looked rusty or sore, and would scrape out a double bogey six, but Pavin had maneuvered his ball into play and slapped it on the green.

After a cursory look for his tee shot, Langer walked to his partner's side. "How far is this?" he asked.

"A hundred twenty-six to the front edge plus twenty-four yards to the pin," Colin replied, looking at his pin sheet. "In other words, a hundred and fifty." Monty felt pleased to be able to give his precise teammate an exact number.

"Where have you taken the yardage from?"

Monty pointed to a sprinkler head.

"Are we talking about the back of the sprinkler head or the front?"

After a moment of incredulity—the circular plastic irrigation cover was nine inches in diameter—Monty realized that Bernhard was not joking. Moments after Colin hit his iron to the green, Mr. German Engineering announced the new rules of the road. Henceforth, only yardage provided by his caddie would be used. Colin and his caddie, Kevin Laffey, would have to consult Pete Coleman for practically every shot. The arrangement made them nervous.

Holes were halved in pars until the 453-yard fourth, the hole that leads the Ocean Course adventure to the edge of the beach. With his bad dream of a grip, Bernhard addressed a forty-foot putt from just over the green. He stared at the ball sternly as it rolled toward the hole. The ball kissed the pin as it fell in. One up for Europe. Montgomerie found it hard to contribute on the front nine; after his first tee faux pas, Langer played way better than his partner or their opponents. Pavin, the master competitor, looked simultaneously frustrated and determined. Pate swung out without flinching, but recalling this match twenty years later, he said, "It hurt."

On the seventh, Steve blasted one of the longest tee balls of the week, a wind- and roll-aided 340 yards. He didn't have to go very hard at a seven iron to get the ball on the green of the 537-yard par five. But a forty-cubic-foot freezer had been buried between him and the hole—or so it looked—and he couldn't quite picture the intricate path to follow. Three putt. Langer had rolled a chip from thirty yards stone dead for a birdie four. Europe moved to two-up.

The helmet of blond hair on Langer's hatless head barely moved in the wind. His face remained a mask.

The par-three eighth was a green plateau in a sea of sand. And insoluble: Any ball landed short hit the bank and died; shots carrying on the surface bounded merrily over and into the sand and seashells. Calcavecchia watched. Reporter Trumpy found him. "It is just so tough out here," Mark said. "Like this little par three. It's just an eight iron, but eight of the best players in the world [everyone in the first two matches] missed the green. That wears on your head."

What about the fatigue? Trumpy asked. It's bad, said Calc: "We got home last night and we were just a bunch of zombies. You're walking around with your tongue on the floor. . . . I needed the afternoon off."

The golfers walked many miles and sweated and stressed, but the most tired man on the grounds never hit a shot. Brett Fischer, the physiotherapist for the American team, had been with Pate at the hospital until the wee hours after the limo accident on Wednesday. Several times a night thereafter, he'd been tiptoeing into the room where Steve and his wife slept, to attach an electrode pad onto the golfer's injured side. Stewart and O'Meara had chronically sore backs, Floyd required work on his thoracic spine, hips, and shoulders, and nearly everyone needed treatment for aching muscles and tightening tendons. The only player who did not stretch was the player with the stiffest swing, Wayne Levi.

"That crash was worse than people realized, and more of our players were hurt than people knew," Fischer recalls. "Corey and Payne had whiplash injuries to the neck but they didn't talk about it because they didn't want to be a distraction. But Steve couldn't hide it. . . . Normally, someone with an injury like his would never play."

Fischer walked with Pate. He'd rubbed analgesic balm on the injured area, wrapped it in an Ace bandage, and secured the bandage with tape. When the strained rib muscle under the bruise began to tighten up, the physio activated a series of heat packs for Pate to press against his side.

He hung in there. Pate made the only pars on holes eight and nine, which squared the match. He bombed another downwind drive three and a half football fields on the tenth hole, but his right hand went unconsciously to his side as he watched his subsequent iron shot drift into the no-man's-land right of the green. Pavin, normally the surest of putters, with a stroke like a cobbler tapping a tack, sawed across a two-footer on the twelfth and missed. Corey finally stepped up on thirteen with an excellent short iron; he and Monty converted short birdie putts. Pate three-putted from three yards on fourteen, then holed from off the green for par on fifteen. Montgomerie answered from ten feet to tie the hole, then exulted, his arms overhead, his face as pink as his shirt. Team Europe took a two-up lead to the seventeenth tee.

The crowd went silent as Monty stepped up to bat with a two iron. His long, ornate swing did not look made for the wind, but thousands of rounds in Scottish gales had taught him a valuable lesson: In a breeze, swing more slowly. Seeing the purity of the strike immediately, European partisans started to whoop before the ball reached its apogee over the lagoon. Loosened eyebrows and a big grin from Monty; his mother would have been proud. Pate pulled his shot into the Sahara. Pavin took four practice swings, two deep breaths, re-teed his ball, then four more practice strokes. He hit a good shot onto the green, but when he failed to make his long putt, and Colin caressed his to within a foot, the match was over.

Woosnam/Broadhurst vs. Azinger/Irwin

World Number One Woosnam evoked the arc of a little Ferris wheel when he hit a golf ball, the clubhead and shaft whirling so fast they made an almost visible circle. The five-foot-four-inch powerhouse enchanted galleries from Augusta to Arabia, but at Kiawah, his work on the greens made them avert their eyes. After resting and practicing Saturday morning, Little Big Man showed up with a new putter, a black-shafted Tad Moore, the model he'd used to win the Masters in April. But still he could not make a putt. That bloody Bermuda grass . . .

World Number Ninety-nine carried him. With amazing sangfroid for a man in his first-ever Ryder Cup match, Paul Broadhurst holed from twenty feet on the third for a birdie three and lipped out a bunker shot on eight. Where had Gallacher been hiding this man, and, more to the point, why? After holing another long putt on ten for another birdie, the wavy-haired Englishman finally celebrated a bit, with a fist pump. The match was even.

After another Broadhurst birdie on thirteen put the Euros one-up, with all four players getting coated like sugar doughnuts by playing in the sand, the match came to seventeen, and Dye Lagoon. The best shot of a bad bunch was Woosie's shot into the Subaru-sized sandpit left of the green. Hale dunked his tee ball; Paul and Paul couldn't do much with nasty shots from way left. With an air of calm in the tense theater, Woosnam splashed out to about eighteen inches. They made him putt it.

Langer/Montgomerie vs. Pate/Pavin

James/Richardson vs. Wadkins/Levi

Perhaps it's a stretch to aver that Langer helped win a match he wasn't even a part of, but you couldn't miss Lanny waiting on fairways and tees with hands on hips, while in the match in front, Bernhard performed his due diligence on every . . . single . . . shot. But it's no exaggeration to state that Wadkins played the Englishmen more or less by himself. Wayne Levi (rhymes with heavy) began the game 5-7-5, bogey, double bogey, bogey, and did not make a birdie all day, or finish a hole for a long stretch in the middle of the round, or help his teammate on any hole until the fifteenth, when his par tied that of James.

Wayne's malaise began on the tee: He had made his bones as a straight hitter, but now his black Yonex driver could not find a fairway. "It's very simple," Jacobsen whispered into his microphone. "Wayne Levi is playing his first match of this Ryder Cup. He's very nervous and has not played well."

If the reports that Levi had not broken 80 in any practice round were true—or almost true—people on the sideline could wonder why he was even playing. Stockton explained: Since every player had to tee up in the Sunday singles, and the singles matches were so important, it made sense to get everyone into battle beforehand. The team matches on Friday and Saturday were four golfers chasing one point; Sunday's twelve singles games involved only two men, so in a sense mano a mano was twice as important.

"Dave's only mistake," says Lanny. "With Pate hurt, and Levi playing poorly, we sacrificed two points by not putting them together." Or one, more like. And although Lanny had proved he could partner with anyone, why not keep him with Irwin? They were, after all, undefeated.

James—his two iron onto the surface at seventeen settled things—basked in the afterglow amid a strangely wonderful background sound. "It's a well-known song," he told Trumpy. "Fans tend to sing it at football games. It's the first time I've heard it at a golf tournament."

Ballesteros/Olazábal vs. Couples/Stewart

Gamesmanship on the seventh hole: With Couples over the green in two but with a putter in his hands, Seve hit a sweet sand shot from twenty-five yards to two feet. Olazábal, with not much at stake, lost his concentration for a moment. His skulled shot from the same sandpit sailed over the gallery and immediately elicited oohs and titters from the audience. "Back, back, back," quipped Rolfing, as if calling a home run. The normally very serious Olly laughed out loud, but he did not take himself out of the hole. It took time for him to locate his ball, and more time for an appeal to replace it (he'd put a definite dent in the cover), and a minute more for him to finally whack a wedge barely on the green in four. The best he could have done, had he holed out from the low trees and the scrub, would have been the four that Seve already had in his pocket. Why bother to go through the charade, if not to ice Fred?

With the Euros still away, now Seve rolled in his shorty for a birdie. If the implacable Couples was supposed to have been unnerved by the delay, it didn't work. His palms on the putter were close to and facing each other, as if in prayer. Clink . . . the ball glided gently through four yards of fringe and five yards of green and into the hole. Couples punched the air. "That's the most excited I've ever seen Fred," said Miller over the roar. "Normally, he's yawning."

More gamesmanship on the ninth hole: Seve killed another tee shot, his usual hook producing yards of roll. Stewart—a long hitter with his irons, but not with a driver—bunted his ball about fifty yards short of Señor Charisma. But as they got to Payne's Titleist, he looked down at it and innocently said, "Dunlop?" It was a joke to call out Seve's brand, but Seve didn't laugh.

Stewart yanked a birdie putt from eight feet on the twelfth; a make would have put his side three-up. And then the match began. Seve hit a short iron close and made the putt for a win on thirteen; Olly, then Payne, created euphoria by holing ten-foot par putts on fourteen. On fifteen, Couples chopped three shots, then holed from the sand to save par. Hosannahs. Seve addressed his twelve-foot putt for birdie, then, hearing distinctly European cheers from a match in front, he stepped away. The moment suitably amped, he made the putt to tie the match. The drama had its own momentum now, and it looked gorgeous, as the setting sun bathed the actors in golden light.

As the other matches concluded, their fans scurried back to watch the epic conclude. Unseen suits in New York told Cirillo to keep rolling. NBC would run an hour and fifteen minutes over its allotted time and show no commercials. So there was adequate air to aim a camera and a microphone at two interesting men in the gallery of the great match, the two captains. Stockton—somber, and contemplating the possibility of defeat for the first time—said he did not regret his decisions regarding Levi and Pate. He'd been camera-shy all week, but now Gallacher was modest and engaging. "I'm pleased some decisions of mine have worked out at last," he said, all straight white teeth and pink skin (he'd given away his hat to a Euro caddie whose face had started to burn). "It's been a tough week for me, I'll tell you. . . . Some of the mistakes of the pairings were on me. They've gotten me out of trouble."

Clicking cameras—or something—caused Olly to back off his putt on sixteen. "Come on!" shouted an impatient (obviously American) fan, the first bit of televised rudeness from the gallery. Seve gestured emphatically at someone in the crowd. Olazábal, then Seve, then Couples missed birdie tries, all on the same line. Still tied. Hundreds of fans sprinted along the sand paths right and left of Dye Lagoon to join the roughly twelve thousand ringing the dreaded seventeenth.

Only Olly and Fred hit the green. Spectators' voices reverberated in the strange acoustics formed by bodies and water and sand. José María missed from ten feet for birdie; Fred holed from six feet for par. Still tied. Cameramen opened the irises of their cameras all the way as the sun reached the horizon and the light faded.

Pars halved the eighteenth. "I don't usually play this much golf in two days, let alone a month," said Fred confusingly on the noisy, darkening green. As she had all day, Deborah Couples had popped out of the gallery to embrace her mate, her giant star-shaped earrings catching the last bit of the sun. After a great deal of hand shaking and hugging, the tired, entertained, drained, optimistic throng receded.

Each team got half a point. This match and the big Match—tied. There was one day to go.

PART FIVE
PURE TENSION AND PANIC

I am delighted to join President Bush in getting today's Ryder Cup play off to a flying start. I'm sure that this round of the great golf battle between Europe and the United States will turn into a classic at Kiawah.

—England's prime minister John Major on NBC, preceding the Sunday broadcast

I hated every moment of it.

—Nick Faldo, after his singles match

Sam Ryder's homely little trophy is turning into a blood prize.

—John Garrity, Sports Illustrated, *October 7, 1991*

15

SUNDAY MORNING, SEPTEMBER 29

The Ocean Course looked orderly and serene from fifteen hundred feet above the beach. Cameras attached to a giant blue-and-white gasbag called the MetLife Blimp zoomed in or peeled back, revealing tiny figures walking two-by-two in the green strips between the marshes and the sand. At intervals, the pairs separated. Blinding light arced around the smaller human: the sun catching a swinging stainless steel shaft. Then the larger form moved back to the side of the smaller one: the caddie and the golf bag reuniting with the golfer. In the sand and scrub on the perimeter scurried twenty-five thousand more miniatures, but spread out more than on any other day this week. Twelve matches to watch instead of four.

The captain held the ship in a hover by keeping the nose pointing into the wind and running the motors. Nothing else but egrets and gulls flew in the lonely Sunday sky, what with the retirement of the blimp's weeklong companion—a prop plane pulling a banner advertising the Crazy Horse Revue.

Traffic increased midmorning, with helicopters and military aircraft obviously patrolling, not ferrying passengers. At ten A.M., an air force jet landed at Charleston Executive Airport, about fifteen miles away from the Kiawah beach. That would be the vice president's plane.

Europe saw that bet and raised a supersonic transport. About ninety minutes later, the team's totally cool ride home circled the course. Players and spectators looked up at the beautiful, futuristic Concorde.

No spectators yet walked on or around the seventeenth, the hole everyone was talking about. From the blimp's-eye view, you saw how the water hazard described the shape of a whiskey bottle. The olive in the uneven bottom of the bottle was the ladies' tee, from which resort golfers would drown innumerable golf balls. This week those few square yards served as the drop area from which chapped-ass golf pros could try again to keep a golf ball dry. The green on seventeen rested against the neck of the bottle, like a long, slender hand ready to pour a drink.

Scanning the ground from the Mount Olympus of the blimp brought home in an intellectual way the severity of the test below. With danger lurking on both sides of virtually every hole, and the utter absence of routine shots, the Ocean could never be a place for your usual game. You could see the way the greens rolled like ocean waves: But how could you figure out such subtle hazards with a crosswind and a two iron in your hands?

It wasn't designed to be easy, said architect Dye. The intense man in tinted glasses told everyone that he'd designed the course for match play, but not everyone heard him. A TV commentator identified "key holes" because that was what he always did when broadcasting a stroke play tournament. But that kind of big thinking didn't apply in a match. The key hole in a match is always this one, then the next one, and at each tee a new mini-tournament commences. The same expert intoned that the absence of birdie holes coming in meant that few players could hope to come from behind to win. Not even remotely true: Between the wind, the baked greens, the roller-coaster golf course, and the heavy breath of the world on each player's neck, pars, bogies, and even double bogies would win holes on the last few holes throughout the Match. You didn't need a birdie, for God's sake. This wasn't the Phoenix Open. On this final day of the Golf War, one player would come back from being five down after nine holes to tie his opponent. Three others—four down, three down, and two down, respectively—took their games to the eighteenth hole.

The east wind freshened to twenty miles per hour, the strongest steady breeze of the week. The engines droned a little louder, the sound carrying away from the golf course and out to sea. Someone had scraped "USA" in giant letters in the beach sand. But—heavy symbolism—the tide came in and washed them away. The Ryder Cup competition looked tranquil from a height in the morning light, but down on the practice ground, tumult lurked.

The night before, Stockton and Gallacher had played poker. Each knew the other guy's cards but didn't know how he'd lay 'em down.

In choosing the batting order for Ryder Cup singles matches, a couple of concepts seemed immutable. You wanted early momentum, so captains often put their meanest but most magnetic man in the side out first (for example, Lanny Wadkins, 1985, and Paul Azinger vs. Seve Ballesteros in 1989). After winning their matches, these fearless and enthusiastic gents could be counted on to grab a hot dog and go back out on the course to cheer on the rest of the team. A captain needed closers, too, players with the guts to perform with the Cup on the line. Final match heavyweights included Nicklaus vs. Jacklin in '69; Nicklaus again in '75 and '81; Tom Watson vs. Bernard Gallacher in '83; Curtis Strange in '85; Strange vs. Ian Woosnam in '89. The goal was a fast start and a strong finish: simple.

The more subtle strategizing occurred in picking the middle matches. Someone not playing well, or a rookie still getting used to the bright lights, might in theory be safely hidden somewhere between two and ten and not do too much mischief. Montgomerie felt pleased on Saturday evening when Gallacher announced he'd be going off third. "I felt safely tucked away," Colin recalled. "You are not going to win the Ryder Cup for Europe from that position but, equally so, you are not going to be the one to lose it."

After Olazábal, then Stewart, holed gutsy putts for par in the gloaming on Saturday, captains and players convened in their trailers to remove their shoes and open a can of lager and talk for a few minutes about the next day. When would you like to go, Nick? Gallacher asked the discouraged kingpin. "Sooner rather than later," Faldo said. In the other trailer a few feet away, a similar drama unfolded, like the who-wants-to-volunteer-for-the-dangerous-mission scene in a war movie. One final time, the captains weighed their options. Both knew the conventional wisdom well enough to know its limits: The time had come for a bit of gambling.

Gallacher made three unexpected bets. To lead off, he selected Faldo, whose putter and attitude were so iced over he hadn't come close to scoring a point. Anointing him to break the tie in Europe's favor was going out on a limb. The European Captain ventured further from the standard strategy by sticking the Spaniards, his two strongest performers, right in the juicy middle. Perhaps they'd make short work of two lesser opponents—but at what cost? With Olazábal off fourth and Seve, seventh, the undefeated and once-tied stalwarts would be unavailable to start the day with a bang, or to end it in glorious victory.

The captains met, traded lineup cards, and bade each other adieu. The pairings were whisked into the media tent, where wise men drank draft beer in plastic cups and contemplated the matchups. Faldo had drawn Floyd, possibly a lucky break for Europe. Although Ray and Freddie had clobbered Nick and Woosie in a match on Friday, Faldo had heretofore owned Raymond. Seve got sore-ribbed Steve Pate; that looked like a certain victory for the Old Country. But Stockton had been unpredictable, too, by sticking his ace, Azinger, in the four spot where he might have been expected to get, say, David Gilford. Instead he would face Olazábal. So Stockton's lone gambit seemed to have been neutralized—unless Zinger won, in which case the captain was a genius.

"A siege mentality was developing at our hotel," Woosnam recalled, but others described the mood at dinner as upbeat, even jubilant. Wow—3½ points out of 4 in the afternoon! As the team dined in Gallacher's suite, Montgomerie repeatedly heard the same useless advice: Calcavecchia is a great front-runner, so don't let him get ahead of you. As if you could play defense in golf. . . . Meanwhile Faldo felt his anxiety rising like floodwater. "I was the most nervous I have ever been," he recalled. "I had trouble getting off to sleep, and I was pacing round the room at four A.M. with my heart going flat out. I thought I was going to have a heart attack."

All was positive in the American dining room, with players telling each other how damn good they were, how tomorrow was going to be their day! But food poisoning, perhaps from the penne pasta, struck Stewart, Azinger, and Beck, and gave them some unpleasant moments.

In the morning, almost three hours before air, techs in the dirigible made sure everything was still working. Down on the ground, in a row of players warming their engines, one man, Pate, had an attentive audience of his caddie, physiotherapist Brett Fischer, and Captain Stockton. Let's zoom in: For about half an hour, the golfer taps, rather than hits, a series of golf balls, as if arthritic or aged. He places his right hand on his left side. He shakes his head. Fischer says something. Pate says something. Stockton says something, then rushes off. Pate sharply yanks the strap on the back of his glove. If we were closer, we'd hear the ripping sound of unfastening Velcro.

Pate would withdraw. By prior arrangement, Gallacher had selected a man to sit out if an American player could not answer the bell. The name in the brown envelope was David Gilford. Each team got half a point for the match not played. Seve slid down a spot in the order to the six spot to go against the man Gilford would have faced: Levi. Gilford was shattered, inconsolable, so badly did he want to redeem his 0-2 record. Several members of Team Europe—probably more—smelled skullduggery. Gallacher expressed his suspicion slyly, by referring to "Pate, who had been hitting the ball a country mile the day before." Well after the fact, Woosnam, Torrance, and Seve committed their suspicions to ink on paper. In his 2010 Ryder Cup memoir, Torrance said:

> To this day, I wonder how hurt Pate actually was. I was in one of the cars that bashed into each other, and it wasn't much of a concertina effect at all. . . . In the second round of fourballs he hit a driver and five iron to get up in two on the par five eleventh. I couldn't get near it in two! . . . To add to our feelings of doubt about the whole thing, it soon emerged that Pate had been drawn to play against Seve [and] then Seve found himself playing Wayne Levi, undoubtedly America's weakest player. That was not a good result for us, because it was a real waste of Seve's point. I reckon anyone on our team could have beaten Levi. . . . We felt it was the Americans who got half a point out of the affair.

Seve's recollections echoed Torrance's. "For me the strangest event of the whole four days occurred after the Saturday four balls [sic], when Steve Pate, who was due to play me in the singles, said he'd badly strained his wrist [sic] in an accident," wrote Seve, a bit vaguely, in *Seve.* "Considering how things were going, it was hard not to think something underhand was going on. And the Americans were right to be afraid of me, for I was playing at my best and finished this Ryder Cup with more points than any other player."

These comments impugned two men with impeccable reputations for integrity and spotless records of fair play over decades of competition. A more likely and plausible explanation is that Pate simply aggravated his injury by playing Saturday. Torrance "wonder[ed] how hurt Pate actually was"? It certainly looked bad. The NBC camera caught a glimpse of the bruise on Saturday: It was big and starkly black on Pate's untanned torso. Recalling September 1991 in September 2011, Pate shook his head ruefully. "It really wasn't much of a decision. I couldn't hit a ball more than forty yards in the air that morning," he said. He didn't tee it up in another competitive round for six weeks, and, he added, stretching a little to one side, "it's still not right."

But Pategate distracted no one, except Pate, Gilford, Seve, and Levi. There simply wasn't time to worry about it. Pate scratched at eight-thirty, and the first game, Faldo versus Floyd, would tee off ten minutes later.

The final chapter of the melodrama began to unfold. The first team to reach 14½ points would swig the champagne and act a fool, and dance around the little gold cup.

Score: Europe 8½, USA 8½

If genius resides in an infinite capacity for taking pains, it found hospitable quarters in the restless personality of Nick Faldo. The sleepless bundle of nerves shook hands with Ray, took a golf ball and a club from Fanny, sorted through a thousand different inputs and variables, and hit shot one down the fairway. He'd told Bernard to put him in early, so he could get the thing over with, but not *first*! He didn't want the pressure. His striking and his putting couldn't be depended on. Nick's internal monologue was not visible, of course, and his uncertainty did not manifest until deep in the round. He made a standard two-putt par on the first hole, a very nice birdie from eight feet on the par-five second, and a bogey on the third—no disgrace on the volcano hole. Floyd looked sharp in the day's uniform of off-white beltless slacks, a white (or red) short-sleeved sweater, and white shirt, hard collar or soft (Ray, Zinger, Calc, and Lanny were hard-collar men). At least Floyd looked good during his bogey, par, double bogey start. Faldo stood three-up after three.

The match between these two old rivals proceeded with a wobbly rhythm, with neither player finding a beat he could dance to. Nick's three-hole lead fell to one. The one-hole lead increased to four, as Faldo made two birdies and an eagle on the front nine. But Floyd, for forty years a golf gambler, knew not to give up or go away. He almost holed his wedge second shot on ten; after conceding the putt, Faldo holed from thirty-two feet (with a four-foot break) to tie. Thrilling! But the stiff land-to-sea, left-to-right breeze from hole fourteen to the house bothered the Englishman more than the North Carolinian. As the kite-flying wind flattened and billowed Nick's uniform of muted blue-green plaid pants and pale blue shirt and perfect hair, his lead shrank to two holes with two to play.

On seventeen, he ran his twenty-foot putt for a two and the win six feet past, and a few cretins in the audience hooted. Before attempting the next stroke—again, to win—Faldo shooed away a TV cameraman and soundman sitting behind him and directly on the line of his putt. A rude subset of the gallery jeered at the slight delay caused by a perfectly reasonable request. Then Nick missed. He'd completed a chilling sequence of a conceded double bogey on the impossible par-three fourteenth, then bogey, bogey, and bogey. Nick was dormie one, that is, one-up with one to play, but not looking good.

Until Ray hit his drive. If Floyd could have whacked his ball into the fairway on eighteen, who knows? But he didn't. We should remember his drive left, into the crowd standing in the sand, because it would be reprised a couple of hours later in the final match of the day. From the unpaved cart path, Floyd punched a ball back into the fairway—all he could do with it. Nick played strong shots into the middle of the fairway and to the middle of the green. His two-putt closed Ray out, 2 and 0. The combatants shook hands, then spoke a few words for the TV cameras. "But these holes are just, and in this breeze, I mean, you know, you stand up on fourteen and wonder what the *hell* you gotta do," babbled Faldo like a crash survivor. "Some of the shots are just not on, the percentages are not on." Floyd seemed more composed. "I'm disappointed I lost," he told the worldwide television audience. "But I hope my comeback can give the other guys some spirit."

Europe 9½, USA 8½

Payne Stewart did not lack spirit. Despite the course management lesson he was receiving from the vulpine little man from Northern Ireland—Feherty—Stewart stayed upbeat. Players on both sides recognized the purity of Payne's love for everything about the Ryder Cup. "Our Seve," says Jacobsen. But as badly as Stewart wanted to win a point, he would not let the game result interfere with the protocols of sportsmanship.

Just as Faldo had done, Feherty started fast: Par-birdie-par-par put him three-up over Payne, establishing a lead he held until a wave of pressure on the fifteenth erupted in a shanked two iron—the shank being golf's most catastrophic shot, a ricochet from the clubface onto the hosel, resulting in a ball that travels east for the player aiming north. The shank is what a sliced artery is to a surgeon. It is golf malpractice, grounds for a lawsuit. Post-shank, poor David lost sixteen to Payne's par: From four-up and an easy win he'd descended to two-up with two to play. Trembling inside, Feherty waded through the soft white sand to the next tee. As he recalled it:

> And I'm walking from the sixteenth green to the seventeenth tee. And the noise at Kiawah was unbelievable. It was Desert Storm, it was Corey Pavin running

> out from behind a sand hill like Rommel with his horrible little knotted fist. The crowd was swept up into a frenzy. And I'm trying to get to the seventeenth, when all of a sudden a huge lady marshal gets in front of me and pokes me right here and says, "Where do you think *you're* going?" What am I, a heavily disguised spectator? I'm wearing cerise pants, for Chrissake, I'm in a Ryder Cup uniform. I'm on my way to lose my mind.
>
> An arm comes across my shoulder and Payne put his face right here, on mine—I can still smell the Red Man [chewing tobacco]—and I could tell that he was grinning like a bucket of French fries. He says, "Ma'am, I'd love for you to hold him here, but he's playing against me." And he swept me up onto the tee in his arms like that. Payne really got the Ryder Cup. Understood what it was all about.

But there was still the little matter of playing seventeen. Into the air thick with pressure—and against a strong breeze—Stewart hit a shot to tighten the noose around Feherty's neck: on the green. Feherty's turn: with a rising gorge, a very large crowd mostly hoping he'd hit it into the water, and a one iron. But this was the greatest day of golf of David's life. He nailed it, a hard shot that started at the sandpit on the left and began to fade back perfectly. "When it was in the air, I knew it was OK," remembers Feherty. "But I look over and see Jacklin, the asshole, still turned away and with his hand over his eyes. He was the only one with less confidence in me than me."

Stewart went for the deuce from thirty, as he had to, and ran it eight feet past. Feherty's exquisite lag from twenty died stone dead. He'd taken down the U.S. Open champion, 2 and 1. He threw an air punch, and then another, slow uppercuts that almost touched the ground and ended over his head.

"That three wood you hit really put the pressure on him," said the TV boy in the aftermath, adopting the technique of an adoring declaration rather than posing a question. "But he dealt with it and hit a great shot," said Payne with grace. "He played better than I did, so he deserves to win."

Europe 10½, USA 8½

The vice president of the United States arrived at the Ocean Course clubhouse with his Secret Service retinue and the Honorable Carroll A. Campbell, the (not coincidentally Republican) governor of South Carolina. "I got there around noon," Quayle recalls. "But I discussed it with someone from the PGA and decided not to go out on the golf course. A collapse was happening [for Team U.S.]. I've played enough golf to know I did not want to go out and add to the pressure." So V-POTUS, the governor, and their posse of seven impassive men in dark suits did what many millions around the world were doing: They watched the end of the Ryder Cup on television.

During the lunch hour, match nineteen—the third singles game—commanded most of the attention. Unbelievable theater: NBC had come on the air too late to show their front nine, so only eyewitnesses had seen Mark Calcavecchia steamroller Colin Montgomerie into the sand. Five down after nine holes, just as Monty's teammates had feared. . . . Calc had birdied one, seven, and nine, making his only miscue—a double on the third, the volcano—barely worth mentioning. The nine-hundred-yard buggy ride from the ninth green to the tenth tee felt like a relief to Monty, and a useful interregnum: "I told myself I would not let Calcavecchia walk all over me any longer." Monty hit two crooked shots on ten, leaving him forty yards left of the hole. From there, from the sand—small miracle—he holed it. Another Montgomerie birdie on eleven brought him to three holes down, but Calc did not show much concern. The American hit a good shot on the rooftop-to-rooftop fourteenth; Colin made a hash of his first, second, and third shots, and conceded the hole. Calc was dormie four.

With his inevitable triumph over Monty, the man with the honor on fifteen would have an enviable record of three wins, one loss in the '91 Ryder Cup. His horrid finish in the singles in '89 would be blurred in memory, if not erased. The proper way to think of Calcavecchia would be restored—he was the clutch performer who birdied two of the final three holes to get into a play-off for the Open Championship of '89, who then birdied two of the final three holes of the four-hole shootout to win the damn thing. The cherry on the top of his sundae that Sunday at Troon was the full five-iron shot he hit to within six feet on the seventy-sixth and final hole, and the subsequent made putt.

"I've always said, 'When it's your turn to win, you win. You're picked,' " he would tell the press while he clutched the Claret Jug. His life peaked again two weeks later, when Sheryl gave birth to Brittney Jo, their first child.

The wind abruptly freshened—left to right and out to sea—

as Calc addressed his tee ball on the high plateau of the fifteenth tee. He owned a uniquely accessible appeal. The other stars striding this acreage were almost not of this world in personality (Faldo, for example) and physiognomy (Couples), but Calc seemed like that unpretentious, likable guy you played high school ball with. He enjoyed bowling, pool, and beer, with a rock music soundtrack. His extraordinary skill at games separated him, of course, from the mass of men. But even for elite performers, athletic performance under pressure is subtle, a delicate balance, and never a sure thing. For Calc, the demons attacked on fifteen. Outlined against the ice blue September sky, his tee ball arced a mile right, into the dunes land, step one on a path toward an apocalyptic triple bogey seven. Monty won with a double. Dormie three.

Same thing on sixteen: Calc's tee ball sailed toward the beach like a suicidal booby. His synapses were shorting. Horrid shots alternated with good ones. Concurrent with a body that moved just a little too fast, and hands unable to synchronize to the altered tempo, his luck deserted him. He nailed his six-iron third shot to sixteen, but it carried *just* far enough to land onto the rock-hard back fringe and hop into the scrub. Bogey to Monty's par. Vice President Quayle had arrived by this time; Calc's match was the ongoing collapse that kept him in the clubhouse and glued to a tube. Dormie two.

And into the cauldron they went. Montgomerie faded the ball, just as Calc did, so this strong, quartering left-to-right breeze stressed him badly. The pin on seventeen seemed set almost in Dye Lagoon, so close was it to the water, way back in the farthest part of the green, near the top of the whiskey bottle.

Monty fussed and squinted at the unbearably narrow and dangerous target, and deep-breathed like an expectant mom in a Lamaze class. About to hit . . . he backed off. About to hit . . . he backed off again. Finally he belted a two iron with that big flowing swing . . . into the reeds and water short and right of the green.

European fans in the sandy amphitheater exhaled. Too bad, Colin. Well done to get this far. All his opponent needed to do now was to aim toward Moncks Corner or any other bit of inland South Carolina—just anything left. The kind of mediocre drive a ten-handicap smacks on the range would do. "He's a fader," Miller told the TV audience. "This hole sets up well for Calc." But rebellious neurons had staged a palace coup in Mark's brain. At this crucial moment, all he felt, he said, was "pure tension and panic."

He aimed way left but didn't employ his usual lofty fade. Instead he tried a virtual trick shot, a low hook. The renegades that had seized the helm in his dorsolateral prefrontal cortex decided that a wind-cheating, left-curving shot would be doubly safe. Right? Wrong. Calc attempted right-to-left shots under pressure as often as it snowed in Charleston, which is to say, very rarely. Into the lightning storm of neural activity in his skull, another saboteur screamed in a helium voice, "You don't have enough club." Constricted and conflicted, Calc swung. His weight never left his left side. His body didn't pivot. His hands delofted the club to zero degrees. The ball splashed directly and shockingly into Dye Lagoon, a hundred yards short of the goal. It was a shank, indescribably ugly, the second one we'd seen in the last few minutes (Feherty on fifteen).

"That might have been the strangest shot by a golf professional I've ever seen, right there," said Johnny Miller. Montgomerie recalled his "utter astonishment."

Through the groaning, moaning, disbelieving crowd the golfers staggered to the drop area, but it was not the one that had been used all week. Calc didn't know this patch of green in the dunes to the right even existed, and neither did the caddies. Yardage? None of them knew; a problem because golf pros can hardly make it to the men's room without knowing the yardage. Frowning Monty, the blond caterpillars of his eyebrows crawling together, selected a six iron. He hit a pretty good shot to about twenty feet left of the hole. He put the club back in the bag, and his caddie, Kevin Laffey, covered it quickly with a towel, keeping the opposition from sneaking a peek. Mark and his caddie, Drake Oddy, guessed incorrectly that Colin had hit seven iron, so that's what he hit. It wasn't enough. He finished about thirty feet short of the flag.

Both men missed their long putts for bogies. The Scot's try for a four rolled close; Calc threw him his ball, conceding the five. His own putt of twenty, twenty-four inches would end this situation comedy, and the match. Montgomerie knew the game was up; slumping, resigned, he handed his glove and the coin he used to mark and his ball to his caddie. He wasn't going to win *another* hole with a double bogey. "I was about to concede the putt, when I thought again," Monty said. "This was a team event and some of the more senior members of the European side would not approve of one of their rookies taking things into his own hands to that degree."

But the nightmare would not end—Calcavecchia missed,

badly, left. More group gasping. Mark walked to the back of the green and dropped his golf ball. One-handed, he hit it gently on the bounce with his Ping putter into the crowd, a souvenir for some lucky fan—and quite a trick. With the same light touch, he pitched his putter toward his bag and caddie Drake Oddy. Dormie one.

Once again the shattered combatants staggered through the buzzing, disoriented gallery. Jacklin approached Monty on the long sandy walk to the eighteenth tee. "If you can stay standing," he whispered, "you'll win this hole." On the tee, Monty looked over at his opponent and noticed his "eerie calm." Blond Afro blowing, Montgomerie took his driver from his caddie and hit one down the middle. The Yank also had supporters in his corner, in teammates Floyd and Stewart. "Come on, Calc, you can do it!" said Raymond. He could—Calc blistered an enough-is-enough drive down the left side and well past Monty. The big man from the little town in Nebraska would take his final full swing with a three iron.

"What a shot!" enthused Ray as the ball hung in the air. But his effort contained no subtlety; it was too aggressive for the situation. On the other hand, maybe it wasn't so bad considering he'd lateraled his previous long iron. At any rate, the ball landed only a few yards from the flagstick, but it was a fighter jet coming in too hot for the carrier deck. From over the green and to the right, Mark hit a mediocre chip not quite over a voluptuous curve—should have putted it, he said later. Monty had played a relatively cautious second shot, but at least he got it on. His long putt to win the hole and tie the match stopped short by the length of a broken tee, resulting in an operatic reaction from Monty, who did everything but sing in Italian.

Now Calc lined up a twelve-foot putt. It was 1:33 P.M. In silence, he tapped the ball. The ball rolled. The ball did not go in. His collapse had been epic. A half point for both sides: Europe had won the hole and tied the match.

"I just knew that half point was going to cost us the Ryder Cup," Calcavecchia recalled. "I couldn't handle it."

Europe 11, USA 9

One day early in the week, Paul Azinger had sat by himself in the team trailer, listening to a recording of "God Bless America." "Jeez, Zinger," Stockton had said. "Don't get *too* psyched up."

Now he stood on the seventeenth tee, the wind rippling the strands in the neat mop of his hair. Azinger's match with Europe's best, the grimly determined José María Olazábal, had been a dogfight, with lots of birdies (seven) and only four tied holes all day. But neither player achieved a lead of more than one-up, and the game stood even with two to play. Raymond and Payne had lost, and Calc had only tied. Something in the wind told Zinger he had to win, just had to.

Olly, with the honor since his par on the impossible fourteenth, hit first. His one iron aimed left would not fade back onto the green. The ball finished its journey in a weirdly difficult spot in the unmaintained sand, but at least it had avoided the pond so recently visited by the match in front.

Now Azinger took the stage. His previous two shots on seventeen had been leaked catastrophically right into the water and overcompensated dead left into the scrub. He selected a club, then initiated a ritual to stave off the creature from Dye Lagoon:

He lifted the neck of his red short-sleeved sweater with his right hand; tossed grass into the air; tugged on his right pants leg; took a practice swing, and another, and another, and another; plucked more grass and threw it into the air; back to the neck of the sweater; extended his left arm; pulled on the left shoulder of his shirt with his right hand; back to the sweater; shirt; the grass again; left arm extension; sweater; arm extension; shirt; shirt; shirt; arm extension; pants.

His penance complete at last, Paul crushed a two-iron shot onto the green. He two-putted from fifty feet to win the hole, and won the next, to take the match two-up. He and Olly hadn't exchanged a word all day, but now Zinger leaned back and closed his eyes and yelled in exaltation.

McCumber: I tell you what, dramatic victory for the U.S.

Azinger: I tell you what, overwhelming the anxiety I felt before the round, before the tournament, during the round. I'm just thrilled it's over, for me anyway. . . . My arms just relaxed for some reason. I just had that relaxed feeling on seventeen tee, my arms, I just let 'em swing down the line. . . . I just thank the Lord because I had that peace of mind. I'm just really thankful.

Calcavecchia did not witness the final act of his relaxed comrade's defeat of Spain. After firmly declining an interview request from Johnny Miller, the physician on call examined Mark, who seemed to be hyperventilating and felt numb in his hands and arms. "Try to relax," the doctor said. Calc walked dazedly down a short path through the scrub to the beach, where the roar of the surf joined the roaring in his head. But the sea sounds did not soothe him. Stewart, solicitous and protective, stayed with him for a time, and then he left, and then Sheryl left. Brett Fischer kept an eye on the shattered man.

"It looked so odd," the trainer recalls. "All the people are over here, and Mark's over there, all alone." Calc sat in the sand and wept. After a while he rolled up his pants and waded into the Atlantic without removing his shoes. But in this insane hour, he did a very sane thing: He asked his wife to go get their two-year-old. He just wanted to hold her.

Europe 11, USA 10

Whither Pate? The wounded warrior walked in the gallery of match twenty-one, the fifth singles game, Pavin vs. Richardson. The UCLA teammates wore plain white hats, with Pate's cap turned backward. "We never even considered that [the camo hats] would offend people," says Pate. "I don't get it."

But watching Pavin? That was easy to get. With his curveballs, punches, and bulletproof short game, Steve's fast-walking, splay-footed little friend played an entertaining brand of golf. And in this match, he entertained more than ever. If that's the word—Gallacher remembered Corey's conduct much differently.

"Hugely demonstrative," the captain would write. "[His] behavior on the final day bordered on the bizarre as he whipped up gallery support by exaggerating every reaction to almost laughing point."

While Bernard may overstate, still, it's impossible to imagine Ryder Cup saints such as Cotton or Hogan or Jacklin or Palmer organizing cheers. Even the matador, Ballesteros, didn't drop the veil until his match had been won, and even then, not too much. But Pavin felt that he was reacting to the unique atmosphere at Kiawah, not creating it.

"The crowds were really vocal," he recalls. "Of all the Ryder Cups I played, it was the most like a college football bowl game. There'd be European fans on one side of a green and Americans on the other, trying to see who could cheer the loudest. A lot of flags were being waved around. It was fun."

And made more fun for the fist pumper when he won the fourteenth and sixteenth holes with pars for a two-up lead. Corey hit a three wood left on seventeen, into a half-plugged lie in the bomb crater, while Richardson hit a superb shot onto the green. Although the jockey-sized Pavin couldn't see the flagstick, he turned a lost hole into a won match with a brilliant chop from the sand. He hopped out of the pit and walked along with the ball as it rolled toward the hole, throwing two uppercuts and a left hook, his joyous shouts drowned out by ten thousand others. He removed his hat, the better to feel the love.

Richardson let him putt the very short one for the 2 and 1 win. Corey drilled it in with his brass Bulls Eye.

Europe 11, USA 11

What a gesture: After stroking a thirty-five-foot putt for birdie on the eighth green, Seve watched for two seconds, then started to walk to the ninth tee. Yeah, he made it.

Confidence or condescension? Probably both motivated Seve. He did not think of Levi as a worthy opponent, and the American's perceived ignorance of the Rules further eroded the respect. Cases in point: On the par-five second hole—his bête noire all week—Seve went back and forth through the marsh and jungle until he lay four, far to the left and far from the green. After two perfect shots, Levi lay two in the fairway. Billy Foster, Seve's caddie, suggested he concede the hole. No, said *el jugador*, let's see what Levi does with his third.

Why oh why oh, Wayne-oh, would you go for this pin? Alone among the participants we contacted, Levi wouldn't discuss his week at Kiawah, and he's not a memoirist, so we'll have to guess the reason the 1990 PGA Tour Player of the Year played for a four when a six would have won the hole. His too aggressive third rolled through the green and into the water. Then, instead of dropping a new ball on the ground opposite where he'd entered the hazard, he took the more severe penalty and hit again from the fairway—and into the drink again. Seve's seven won the hole.

On the ninth green, Levi putted up to about a yard from the cup and said I'll finish. Oh, no, you won't, replied Seve, not without my permission. *¡Jesucristo!* Didn't he know Rule One of match play—that you control your opponent's ball? In fact Wayne didn't know, and called for an umpire, who said, predictably, that Seve was right. At which point Señor Charisma holed another birdie putt—this one from ten feet—to go three-up.

Levi showed grit by fighting back to extend the match to the sixteenth. He also putted. Very. Slowly. Each hole they played was another hole Seve would not be available to inspire his teammates, and in everyone's mind on both sides, that was a real thing. Moments after the handshakes, Gallacher was in Seve's ear, giving his coach on the field an update and marching orders. Seve seemed not to notice the *beso* Carmen planted on his cheek. His gaze was outward now. He would add his intensity to the coolness of Gallacher, a one-two coaching punch that would surely bring home a winner.

Europe 12, USA 11

The wives suffered as coaches do, feeling simultaneously helpless to affect the outcome of their husbands' matches, and at least a little responsible for it. The red-white-and-blue-draped U.S. spouses—Gallacher said a bit unkindly that the gung-ho American wives looked like aging chorus girls—had the bulk of the crowd behind them. They kept their dignity most of the time, but Deborah Couples, an attention hog of the first order, waved a little flag and skied in her husband's wake. The Euro wives surely endured more in their long walks around the Ocean. Jane James, Carmen Ballesteros, Lorraine Broadhurst,

Gill Faldo, Suzanne Torrance, Vikki Langer, Glen Woosnam, and the others blended much more than the American gals, in relatively subdued outfits that complemented the color schemes of their husbands' uniforms. Certainly they overheard someone at some point say, "Miss it, you English/Welsh/German/Scottish/Spanish/Republic of Northern Ireland bastard." According to Woosnam, several times his and his mates' mates suffered through "unpleasant incidents" with American partisans—one more thing about this Ryder Cup Woosie absolutely hated.

Chip Beck gave him another.

Their match crackled with intensity, for both Beck (0-2, and a captain's pick) and Woosnam (1-2, and the top-ranked golfer in the world) had disappointed. Now they bore down and played by far their best stuff of the week. On the crazy-hard course, two crazy shots by Beck won him the match. With Ian up close for a birdie on eleven, Beck skidded a short but blind sand shot into the hole for an eagle three and a one-up lead. Woosie could have, should have, squared the match on fourteen, when he hit the impossible green, and Chip chipped twice and still hadn't made the surface. Then, incredibly, Beck lobbed one into the hole from down below, the equivalent of getting a ball to stop on the ridgeline of a roof. Woosnam could have kicked himself after he three-putted to tie the hole.

Into the claustrophobic pressure, Beck hit a hold-your-breath three wood on seventeen to about fifteen feet past the flag, a shot to savor forever. With Woosie in difficulty in the sandy mess left of the green, Chip's gentle putt to within an inch won the hole, par to bogey, and the match, 3 and 1. "I did what it took, and I'm really happy about that," he told TV's purple-shirted Trumpy, tapping the giant ex-football player in the chest for emphasis. "I just needed to redeem myself and I needed to do it today."

Europe 12, USA 12

John Garrity of *Sports Illustrated* and *Golf World*'s Gary Van Sickle tapped computer keys, scratched notes with pens on paper, and looked up at TV monitors while wondering if it was time to go outside the tent again. As the two top "game story" writers in the odd world of golf journalism, they routinely faced a difficult challenge: to tell the story of a tournament with enough drama and insight so that readers who had already seen the thing on television would also want to read about it. This week the task was harder than usual, owing to the lack of media access to the actors in the play. And the behavior of their peers from Europe distracted and annoyed American writers for whom the phrase *no cheering in the press box* was an article of faith.

In his review of the week in *Golf World*, Van Sickle commented on the lack of professionalism of the ink-stained Londoners, Glaswegians, and Düsseldorfers. "Outright cheering. . . . It was stunning," Van Sickle recalls. "They let out a huge yell when Calc hit it in the water. I mentioned that in my story, but now that I think about it, those guys may all have had bets down. They may have been rooting for the money."

Garrity and Van Sickle had done many exhausting laps around the Ocean on Friday and Saturday, enough to know that covering the twelve-ring circus of the singles matches would require them to remain close to a TV. But now, with the end drawing near and the result still totally up in the South Carolina air, both men hiked out to watch the denouement. Neither writer recalls watching Paul Broadhurst's efficient 3 and 1 dismantling of Mark O'Meara. The match ended in anticlimax, with Mark putting two balls in Dye Lagoon and then surrendering. The Englishman had won two out of two matches. The same thought occurred to many observers: Why hadn't Gallacher played Broadhurst more?

Europe 13, USA 12

As each match drew down to its conclusion, the gallery for the remaining games increased. Most of the event's thousand volunteers and seven hundred media added to the crush of the twenty-five thousand with tickets. That Olympic hockey game chant—U-S-A! U-S-A!—resonated with every positive result for the home side. As the sun began to slant in the afternoon sky, spectators, TV watchers, TV announcers, and players felt the paralysis of pressure in varying degrees.

But not Bob. In the middle of the warm afternoon, Bob Owca (pronounced oak-uh) finally got to the Ryder Cup. Although the well-met front-desk man at the Kiawah Island Inn was exhausted from working the night shift all week, he couldn't miss the opportunity to see at least some of the great event. Arriving at the Ocean at about one o'clock via shuttle bus, Owca looked for a suitable location to take his ease, triangulating beer tent, restroom, and a handy exit. A level spot at the edge of the eighteenth green fit the bill. He could soak up sun and suds and the atmosphere without being unduly bothered by crowds. After the Calcavecchia match came through, Bob was more or less alone again. There was no giant TV screen for match information; he relied instead on intelligence provided by passing aficionados. No other match made it to eighteen. Until . . .

Match twenty-six—the tenth singles game—pitted Torrance against Couples. Sam had had indifferent results this week—a tie and a loss with Feherty—but thanks to '85, his status as a Ryder Cup hero would never be in jeopardy. Couples, on the other hand, still had a lot to prove. For years he'd been a compelling figure, with shoulder ligaments so loose he appeared to be double-jointed, and timing so sweet he seemed to hit every shot with maximum force, especially with the big shillelagh, his persimmon MacGregor Tommy Armour 845 driver. Also, he looked like Paul Simon with hair. He'd only won a couple of times—no majors—but in this Ryder Cup, he'd asserted himself. Was he the new best player in the United States? He'd be in the conversation if he didn't stub his toe against Sam of the Broom Handle.

The Torrance putting method was as weird as Langer's and had been motivated by the same existential dread of short putts. The twitches began, Sam said, on the eighteenth green at Muirfield Village in the '87 Ryder Cup. With two putts from fifteen feet to win the hole and tie his match with Larry Mize, the Scot's hands began to shake uncontrollably. They didn't seem to even belong to him. Somehow, he rolled the putt up to within a few inches and won his half-point, but severe damage had been done. Torrance had the yips, or the virus that causes yips.

Two years and many, many misses later, when Torrance was "back home in Largs, I remembered the long putter, and climbed onto the snooker table—as you do." In his groundbreaking procedure, Sam grabbed the top of the handle on the long shaft in his left palm and placed it directly under his chin, then put his chin on the little Señor Wences cavity formed by his thumb and index finger. To say it was weird doesn't capture the incomparable oddity of the Torrance technique.

Sam had penalized himself when his ball moved as he addressed it on the eleventh fairway, and that lost hole put him four down. But, sixteen-hole long story short, his baroque putting style let him down. In an ironic finish, he holed from twenty-odd feet for par on sixteen. Could have used that earlier, but now Fred had only to negotiate from half a yard to tie, and win the match—a putt he handled without incident.

The crowd whooped, Fred smiled, said nothing very interesting in the TV interview, and Deborah hovered annoyingly. Two matches remained, and the home team was going to win both. Good time for the chant: U-S-A! U-S-A!

OK, everyone get off the green, turn around, and let's watch the end of Wadkins vs. James. Lanny led.

USA 13, Europe 13

Mr. Wadkins would like to describe the best shot he hit all week. The matter of good-better-best shots was a tricky one, of course, because the Ocean demanded extraordinary performance for the merest thing, such as hitting a green in regulation. In this strong wind, the par threes on the second nine required shots even the best in the world could not usually summon.

Their game had been dodgeball on the outbound nine, with Lanny throwing a barrage of pars that the resolute James could not evade. And when Wadkins stumbled, James staggered: The Yank won the ninth with a bogey to go four-up.

Perhaps the thought began to form on the midround road trip from the ninth green to the tenth tee in a Club Car Model DS-IQ electric golf cart, whose rustproof frame of aircraft-grade aluminum made it ideal for coastal environments. While cruising in the DS-IQ on the sand path past the tents and the practice range and the people, Lanny realized he did not want to play the seventeenth hole again. Not today. Especially not today.

James won the tenth with a par and LW lipped out a short putt to lose thirteen. No matter the state of the match, arrival at the fourteenth caused hard swallowing. An hour and a half earlier, Faldo had stood near his teed-up ball for two solid minutes while wondering just what the *hell* to do. But the mustachioed James, with a bit of momentum now, banged a four wood onto the wind-blown mesa—an excellent stroke.

Lanny responded with his best shot of the Cup—a head-high two iron that sizzled as it left the clubface. The ball cut through the breeze and surmounted the hill and stopped just off the surface. His chip provided dessert after that delicious entrée: "I took a six iron, downhill, downwind. It rolled down, did-dit-dit, and *just* fell in the edge." Back to three-up for Lanny.

Seve oversaw the re-placement of James's ball after someone accidentally kicked it behind the sixteenth green, but he could not inspire a different outcome. Wadkins won 3 and 2, accomplishing both his missions, earning a point and avoiding the tee shot on seventeen. The instant the beautiful brown-haired Peni embraced her husband, all the emotion and effort of the week overcame him. It was a little strange to see the fierce competitor cry. "I don't know if I've ever worked harder," Lanny told the camera and the microphone, and then he broke down again.

After all this—six days on the wild, charming island, twenty-seven matches, a limo crash, Michael D, indignation, brilliance, abject failure, chanting, seafood, psych-outs, and soccer songs, the result was still in doubt. If Hale won or halved, the United States won. If Hale lost, the match would be tied, and Europe would retain the Cup.

"Retain the Cup" literally: When the teams tied in 1969, the gold trophy had spent a year here, and a year there. But following the tie of '89, and the sharp increase in the value of the little statue, it had stayed in Europe all twenty-four months. Neither side wanted another stalemate, but the U.S. side didn't want it more.

Pure tension and panic filled the air. It radiated out of TV screens. Sean Connery, George Bush, Dan Quayle, Queen Elizabeth II, John Major, Stockton, Gallacher, Seve, Zinger, and millions more leaned into it.

The final act was a bit bizarre.

USA 14, Europe 13

With due respect to the Wadkins wedge in '83 and the Torrance putt in '85, of all the shots hit in all the Ryder Cups, three stand out above the others. One of them wasn't really a shot: It was Nicklaus picking up Jacklin's coin, conceding what would have been a nerve-wracking two-foot putt, the generous gesture that enabled the Tie of '69. The second immortal stroke had been struck earlier this day. Calcavecchia's shank on seventeen symbolized the terror of this course, the paralyzing pressure of this particular Cup, and how much things had changed since Jack gave Tony that putt. The third shot that will live forever was about to be hit by Bernhard Langer.

The anchorman for Europe was not an expressive man. Self-control paved the road to his virtuous life and his world-class golf game. Bernhard's poker face made him discouraging to play against, but he was no robot. He reacted to a chip-in at the '87 Cup with a yogic back bend leading to a joyous flop in the soft Ohio grass. The humiliations his putter caused had also cracked his stoicism. Torrance, an expert in the field of missed putts, recalled seeing "the poor German kid in tears" over his work with the flat stick at the Hennessy Cognac Match at Lille. At the British PGA of 1982, Sam watched as Bernhard smacked a fifteen-foot putt on a flat green clean off the putting surface. But Langer's relentless practice led to a very efficient putting game, an odd grip, and no reason to cry.

His equal in competitive ice was his opponent, Hale Irwin. Read, react, tackle, intercept the ball, or bat it down: Twenty-five years after his last game it was easy to imagine Hale with shoulder pads and the number 10 on his black, white, and gold University of Colorado jersey. Irwin had an athlete's easy grace and swagger, but something—perhaps his closed-off on-course persona—kept him from real popularity. Then two things made him lovable: He traded in his nerd glasses for contacts; and the sheer, humanizing joy of his around-the-green high-fiving of everyone with a hand after he holed a long putt that got him into a play-off for the 1990 U.S. Open, which he won.

Four iron, not enough; a poor pitch; three putts. Langer's double bogey on fourteen doubled Irwin's lead to two holes. After Bernhard's putt from two yards lipped out, his arms and shoulders drooped for an instant, then he strode stone faced to the next tee. Irwin had gotten away with murder, a win with a bogey. But as the course swung back along the beach to the clubhouse, all the holes were long, and all played into the howling, left-to-right-and-against wind. Langer's hooks penetrated, while Hale's fade faded in the heavy, salty air.

"I was not striking the ball real purely that week," Irwin would recall. "Downwind I could take my little deflections and play them just fine. I thought I had the advantage downwind. He had a certain advantage playing into the wind."

Fifteen: As the Wadkins/James match marched to its conclusion one hole ahead, Irwin drove way left. He whacked his second from the desert to the middle of the fairway, ninety yards short of the green on the 438-yard (playing 498) par four. He didn't get his third close, and didn't make the thirty-foot putt. Langer, meanwhile, had hit two stinging hooks, the second of which flew precisely over the flag. His third wiggled from the back edge to within six feet, then, with infinite care, he stroked a putt with such perfect speed and direction that it didn't hit the sides as it fell in. One noticed the modest-looking leather-banded watch on his left wrist, worn below the terminus of his ulna. He used a Ping Anser putter with a rubber grip. He didn't wear a hat.

Irwin, one-up.

On sixteen, the par five, most of both teams ringed the green. Behind them stood a metal TV tower—an aiming point—and a large audience, smelling of Skin So Soft and reeking of tension. Hale waited in the fairway for the end of the hubbub at the conclusion of the James/Wadkins match. Hale had hit another drive short and into the sand on the left, and now he would be playing his third from way back, 188 yards into that nasty wind. Seve and Olly stood as Irwin swung . . . not a good one. Irwin's iron started at the tower, then sliced sharply right. The ball bounced off a mound farther right and into the gallery. At least it was a better spot than the giant sandpit on the left.

Woosnam, a man with no shortage of dark accusations regarding this Ryder Cup, would later swear that someone kicked, threw, or otherwise propelled Irwin's ball from the sand and into the grass. Doubtful: The tape shows the ball coming to earth on grass, which undermines Woosie's testimony. "I saw the ball land at the top of a sand dune," he wrote. "I looked away for a few seconds, then turned back to see the ball sitting in the middle of a hollow, pin high, right of the green, in a decent lie." The tape also shows Woosnam smiling in the moments after Irwin's shot, sitting next to Seve and in front of Fanny, and not gesturing or raising a fuss about an injustice.

Now Langer played his third, from 138 in the center of the fairway—wearing a white visor now, and choking way down on an iron. In swing or strategy, something went wrong. NBC producer Cirillo wisely showed tight reaction shots of Seve—deeply concerned—and Bernhard—muttering. He'd gone a little left and a little short, into the eight-foot-deep pit of sand.

Irwin played first, a brilliant chip with spin that hit into the bank then expired, like a car running out of gas, three feet from the hole. Irwin ran to the ball, shook his right hand as if he had dice in there, and emitted the smallest of smiles. "I thought perhaps this is the hole where we might be able to end it," Hale recalled. All he needed was a tie in his match, remember, for the United States to reclaim the Cup.

"I really didn't think he could get up and down," Irwin said. "But that shot he played from the bunker was just fantastic. You can't ever count out a player of Bernhard Langer's stature." Steady as a rock, Langer holed from six feet for his five. Irwin handled his nervous three-footer, but with less aplomb than Bernhard. Now the throng began to sprint to seventeen.

Irwin, one-up.

Both played without delay on seventeen, as if wishing to get the tightrope walk over with. A more frightening moment for Hale, perhaps: "If you flared it off to the right, you were dead [in the water] and I was hitting a lot of flares, believe me."

Both hit creditable shots: away from Dye Lagoon, but not so far left they'd have to deal with the crapshoot of playing their second from the sand and scrub. Just as Irwin's three-wood shot landed, some miscreant in the gallery threw a ball—reportedly a Top Flite—onto the green. Nice throw too: the Spalding ball rolled to about fifteen feet from the hole, and the American fans went bananas. "I knew it wasn't mine," Irwin says.

Calcavecchia had joined his teammates in the gallery. He looked bloodless, as if he'd seen a ghost, and maybe he had. Stewart kept a protective hand on his friend's back as they walked along the lagoon to the green.

Both balls had finished about hole high to the left, off the surface—but with the firm ground and a water hazard on the other side of the hole, these were definitely shots for a putter. Hundreds of spectators moved *onto the green*—unprecedented!—to observe the climax.

Langer first: From off the green, or from long distance, he did not use his octopus grip. He rolled the ball down the barely discernible hill, caught the almost invisible break to the right, and finished four feet away.

Now Hale: too hard, eight feet past. His try to win the Match rolled irresolutely toward the hole but not in it.

Now Langer: Could this basket case of a putter—look at his grip!—make another? He could, and did. Tiny fist pump from Bernhard! The twenty percent of the live audience with European accents went nuts, while the rest groaned and sprinted to the final, final hole. Stockton looked stricken.

Match even.

If Langer won eighteen—and that was plainly the trend—the Match would be tied. Team Europe would party around the trophy like druids around a tree, and the home team and its fans would force a smile and then walk quickly home with its hands in its pockets and its head down.

On the tee, as officials sought order on the course, the superfit Langer took practice swings. He looked a bit like his hero, Gary Player: a golfer with the build of a gymnast. With a wood, he drove perfectly into the crescent-shaped fairway. This was a transition era in golf equipment. As we've seen, one irons, probably the coolest clubs ever, still protruded like long butter knives in some golf pros' bags. Metal woods were catching on, but the manufacturers sized and shaped them like the clubs they were replacing. And golfers anchored themselves in the ground with ferrous spikes, not plastic, and this detail of footwear was about to make a difference.

With a metal driver, Irwin again steered maddeningly hard to port, on the same line Floyd had taken two hours earlier, and about ten people deep into the gallery.

Mark Rolfing, NBC foot soldier: Oh, this ball's *way* left. This ball is headed into the crowd to the left. It'll need to spit out.

The river of people overflowed its banks and filled the final fairway. When, after a struggle, Irwin, Langer, and Rolfing got through the humanity, they found a surprise.

Miller: Now, Hale's ball, if it wasn't for the gallery it probably rolled into the dunes, isn't that correct?

Rolfing: I think so, Johnny. I never saw it come out, then all of a sudden when we got out here it was in pretty good shape. It's actually just in the edge of the fairway.

Langer didn't raise the obvious question then or in *My Autobiography*, but he did at a Champions Tour event in Texas in 2011. "Irwin hit a snap hook," he says, "forty yards at least to the left." Rising from his chair in the locker room at the Woodlands Country Club, Bernhard turned to face the window. "I mean, if that's the fairway"—he gestured to the club's driveway—"he hit it way over there." Bernhard pointed thirty degrees left.

Could the ball have hit someone on the head? Golf balls bouncing off skulls can travel an amazing distance. No. Langer fixed his guest with unbreakable eye contact. "It didn't hit anyone on the head," he said.

In fact, the ball struck Kathy Jorden in the back. Ms. Jorden—what were the odds?—worked in the media department for the PGA of America. Just ahead of her walked PGA of America president Dick Smith; he was carrying the Ryder Cup, following the final match so that the Cup would be on hand the moment the outcome was decided. Because of the swarm of people and an intervening dune, no one on the tee could see the ball on the ground. NBC's camera on a crane showed the little pill in the air, and the surprise of three kneeling white-hatted officials—surely they were in the rough—as the ball returned to earth into the people behind them. Miller used a little wand called a telestrator to indicate that Irwin's ball was back here, in the sand, while Langer's was up there, in the fairway.

"I was just inside the rope, in the rough, not in the sand," recalled Jorden, then thirty-one, and the PGA's manager of broadcasting. "We stopped walking just as Irwin was about to hit. Then we heard 'Fore!' and I turned away. It hit me on the small of the back, on the left side, just above the waist, and bounced off."

Balls colliding with soft tissue don't rebound very far but this ball somehow finished in the short grass. Langer's implication that the ball's journey to the fairway was not an accident is almost unbearable. Golfers revere the Rules to the point of capitalizing the *R*. TV's eagle eye revealed no throwing or kicking or foot hockey body language, and the very idea of a cover-up or a conspiracy of golf ball kickers is laughable.

Yet Langer, the soul of rectitude, is adamant that *something* happened to that ball.

"No way!" says Mike Bylen, Lanny's friend. "I was there. Gravity took it down. Tell Bernhard that I go to church too. I worship the same God."

Irwin felt no surprise that his ball was lying well. "There was not a lot of rough there, just grass or sand," he recalls. "I do remember thinking that I might have been better off if the ball hadn't hit anyone. I was so far back I couldn't reach the green."

The crowd settled. The somber crash of ocean waves made the only sound. Hale had about 225 yards to the center of the green, wind against and quartering to the right. With his familiar wristy swing the Zen master of the fairway wood produced a high fade, a defensive shot, same as on seventeen. He'd have a long pitch to the hole from the right of the green, but at least he'd avoided the sand.

Thirty-five paces closer to the goal, Langer consulted for long moments with his curly-haired caddie, Peter Coleman. They discussed yardage, wind speed and direction, hole location. The main visual was sand and people; as was typical at the Ocean, the target was more suggested than framed. "He's hit a rocket!" said Rolfing as the ball exploded off Langer's three iron. Bernhard's ball landed on the right front of the green and bounced to about a yard off it.

Again—we always see this at the final hole of the Open Championship—the amped-up audience surged onto the final fairway. "It looked like the cavalry coming through," recalls Bob Owca, whose few minutes of solitude were abruptly transformed to a front row seat to this sliver of golf history.

Let's count the number of n-words in Irwin's description of the moment:

"Can we really describe the amount of tension in the air? I was nervous. Flat out, I was nervous. I've been nervous before but in a different kind of way. Absolutely was I nervous. Bernhard was nervous."

It was nervousness—aka choking—that caused Irwin to fluff his chip only halfway to the pin. Hale looked to the sky; a woman in the gallery behind him put her hands on her face and gasped, in unconscious imitation of *The Scream,* the Edvard Munch painting. Was Irwin about to lose three of his final four holes—and the Ryder Cup? By the side of the green, the three-time U.S. Open champ crouched like a baseball catcher and cupped his hands over his eyes. "I couldn't breathe, I couldn't swallow," he admitted a couple of minutes later. . . .

Langer stalled, by asking for relief from a sprinkler head in his line to the hole. He knew the Rule—the obstruction had to interfere with stance or swing, which it didn't. Tension fell like rain.

Too hard, Langer putted just by the edge of the hole about two yards past.

Irwin's irresolute par putt from about thirty feet came up roughly a foot and half short. Langer conceded it. "I thought he was close enough," says Bernhard. "I didn't think of not giving it to him. And I was going to make mine."

Now the final, excruciating stroke:

In the handful of U.S. team dinners and meetings before the Cup began, the main strategic decision had been to not worry too much about going into the sand off the fairway. Often the ball was quite playable. A minor strategic point had been brought up by Irwin. He'd played more practice rounds than anyone else. "Being the old guy, I wanted to make sure I held my weight," he said. "The one thing I gleaned from those practice rounds was that the grain on eighteen was stronger from the back to front than it was on any other hole on the golf course.

"I remember watching him [Langer] putt and thinking, I hope he doesn't know what I know."

Langer and Coleman walked back and forth and around and around. Grain—the direction grass grew—was not the topic of conversation. They talked about spike marks. Two little dirt statues stood in the line to the hole. Three matches had made it to eighteen before this one; judging by the putts they had and the paths they walked, the marks could well have been from the nails on the soles of the Stylo shoes of Stylo's worldwide spokesman, Nick Faldo.

The conferees agreed that the putt broke a bit right, but that a firm putt straight at the left center of the cup would go in without having to risk the uncertain effect of those bumps.

Silence. Ocean sounds. Langer: "I prayed for courage, strength, and a quiet hand. When I hit the putt, I felt it was a good stroke. I thought I had made it."

AFTERWORD

"The most pressure I've ever felt. The worst fun I've ever had."

—*Peter Jacobsen, on the Ryder Cup*

In an unbearable, terrible second the ball rolled to the hole. In a second split it kissed the right lip. Langer's body froze in pain. Inside the amphitheater of sand, the whole world erupted.

Calcavecchia's caddie, Drake Oddy, leapt with everyone else but not high enough or quickly enough. "Is it in?" he shouted. "Is it in?" And then he observed Toni and Paul Azinger kissing atop a sand dune, and he gave Van Sickle a high five that almost broke the writer's left hand.

The recumbent hotelier Owca also missed the money shot. "After Irwin scuffed his chip, I thought it was over. I was sure that Bernhard would make his," he says. "Someone got in front of me just when he hit his putt. Then I got caught up in the moment. People hugging each other, slapping each other on the back, jumping . . ."

The green became Times Square on VE Day. Green glass champagne bottles materialized, their contents sprayed, poured (mostly on Stockton), and chugged. Stewart got in the center of several giddy group hugs, holding his bottle high overhead, like a torch. At some point, he whispered fervently to Calcavecchia that *his* half point today had been the difference. The chanters of U-S-A! U-S-A! let loose.

"Get anyone!" Cirillo yelled into the earbuds of his foot soldiers. "Literal pandemonium," recalls Jacobsen. "I didn't even know if I was on the air." He corralled Calc, who said that in the previous hour he had felt as bad as he could feel but now, much better. Rolfing got Stockton, who observed how close the Match had been; by his side, the captain's lovely wife, Cathy, breathed as if she'd just run a 440—and won. Irwin, who had hugged Langer immediately after the Big Miss, spoke sincerely of his respect for his opponent. In a few moments Hale would make his way to the jam-packed bar in the clubhouse, where he'd catch the eye of Ben Wright. The announcer procured a tumbler of Dewar's for the shaky victor, who tossed it back like a sailor on leave.

Darkness descended in the Team Europe trailer. Seve and Jacklin, emotional men, wept openly. Tears also stood in the eyes of Faldo, Langer, and some of the wives and caddies. Gallacher felt like crying but decided that he couldn't allow himself to break down. Olazábal smoldered, enraged rather than lachrymose. Monty and his wife observed an odd vignette: Vikki Langer turned on the TV, which showed the frolicking and exuberance taking place a few yards away. "We can be doing without that," said Torrance, and flipped it off. But Vikki wanted to see; she turned on the telly again. Then Woosnam found the spectacle of the Americans' party more than he could bear, so he pressed the off button. Vikki, amazingly, turned it back on.

"Eimear and I were still in our corner for the final installment," recalled Montgomerie. "With an almighty thump, one of our number made bloody sure that the TV was finished for good."

Woosnam climbed atop a table—the five-foot-four-inch Welshman always seemed to be climbing on tables. "Come on, guys," quoth Woosie. "This is only a temporary setback. We can put everything right in two years' time."

Drinks were drunk, clothes were changed, composures regained, and the teams convened for the presentation ceremony. On the dais on the practice range, Gallacher shook hands with the vice president and gave him a little lecture: "Even if it was undiplomatic, I told Dan Quayle . . . that I wanted to remind him that we in Britain and in Europe had had servicemen killed in the Gulf War too." Quayle, who hadn't seen what Bernard had seen this week—and hadn't just lost the Ryder Cup—looked bewildered.

"You came here to play the game of golf, and you did it with skill, dignity, and dedication," Quayle said from the stage, not exactly Churchill, but it got the job done. After the captains spoke, and Stockton formally accepted the Cup, the VP ducked out to tear off his tie and put on golf shoes. He and Governor Campbell and the seven Secret Service agents sprinted to the summit of the tenth tee, to squeeze in nine holes on Pete Dye's roller coaster before it was too dark to see.

At this point, someone—probably Stewart—suggested the beach as the perfect backdrop for a team photo. Given the American tradition of soaking the winning coach, what happened next was inevitable: The giddy winners waded in the water for a full-immersion baptism of Stockton. "That had to be Payne's idea," says Wadkins. "I ruined a pair of four-hundred-dollar shoes." Beck laughed and hung back, protecting his beautiful Ryder Cup clothes from the saltwater. "Y'all are crazy!" he yelled.

The after-party confused American fans, who suddenly became the title character in *How the Grinch Stole Christmas.* You remember the story: After he swiped all the gifts from every Who down in Whoville, the green meanie listened for their wailing on Christmas morning . . . "But the sound wasn't sad!/Why, this sound sounded merry!/It couldn't be so!/But it WAS merry! VERY!" Instead of lamenting and staring into their beer, the European fans sang. They sang any happy thing, including a selection from *Mary Poppins,* "Chim Chim Cher-ee." And when Torrance, Woosnam, and—surprise—Langer entered the tent, they received a tremendous ovation. There's a photo somewhere of Bernhard smiling through the post-Match pain. He's above the crowd—on Woosie's shoulders.

The teams dined together that night, the final act in the play. By all reports, the (poorly named) Victory Dinner at the Kiawah Island Inn was a pleasant occasion, with Woosnam, in particular, providing comic relief. As after-dinner mints melted in mouths, the powerful little Welshman picked up Corey Pavin and carried him onto the bus like a baby with a mustache, and then he took the driver's seat and started to drive off. Gallacher noted how somber the three previous valedictory meals had been, because unlike his chaps, the Americans "take defeat so badly."

At ten the next morning, Concorde's engines revved and its afterburners screamed. Team Europe left Charleston, and the Ryder Cup, behind.

What had we just seen? What did it all mean?

The further the '91 Ryder Cup recedes into memory, the more the idea persists that it represented a turning point. Some indefinable test had been passed; the Ryder Cup became a Big Thing and an event never to be missed—not quite the World Cup or the Super Bowl, but in there with Wimbledon and the World Series.

Dollars and cents tell the story pretty well. Let's start with that ten-thousand-acre barrier island off the South Carolina coast: Heretofore underappreciated Kiawah Island appreciated by millions, if not billions. "It put us on the map," says everyone at the resort. Affluent golf nomads couldn't resist the chance to try to hit the green on seventeen, and try to make Langer's putt on eighteen. Many visitors were enchanted by the totality of the experience: that drive on Bohicket Road, the views, the people, the beach—and bought their piece of Kiawah. Eventually the lovely but small Inn was razed; in its place is the Sanctuary. It is magnificent. Five good courses dot the island now. At the top is the Ocean. Architect Dye has returned three times over the years for tweaking, but the Ocean has not lost its terror. In its March 2007 issue, *Golf Digest* declared it to be the toughest track in the world.

The 1991 event also ushered in an era of affluence for the

Ryder Cup's owners. The Sunday broadcast achieved an overnight Nielsen rating of 3.8—damn good when the competition was pro football, and way better than *The New York Times* had predicted the show could achieve. The money and attention snowballed. Including its $13 million rights fee from NBC, the '99 Ryder Cup produced a staggering gross revenue of $63 million, according to *Golf Digest.* Estimated profit: $23 million, with none of the then-standard $7 million deduction for prize money, of course.

All that financial success led like a laser beam to a brief era of bad feeling with the players. Important participants named David Duval, Tiger Woods, and Tiger's best friend/poodle O'Meara—playing Tony Blair to Eldrick's George W. Bush—wondered aloud why the actors in the drama only got babysitter money. The distasteful dispute—millionaires kvetching about their pay!—threatened to derail the Cup's wonderful vibe.

"You should come and donate your salary that week too," O'Meara said with leaden sarcasm in a press conference. "You guys wouldn't mind doing that, would you?"

The sports pages were awash in the buzz-killing arcanum of licensing fees, digital rights, sponsorship, and corporate hospitality. Davis Love III owned a more nuanced understanding of the benefits to everyone if prize money remained something for all the other professional golf tournaments, but not this one. Love spoke out forcefully against playing for pay. A PGA of America official commented that the players did not know the difference between net and gross. But the current system brought back the love: Now each player and the captain designate a charity to receive $200,000. There's still no pay, just a $7,500 honorarium.

Another interesting ray emanating from the post-'91 Ryder Cup sun had to do with publishing. Of the Americans in the side, only Azinger could get a book deal, and that had a lot to do with his inspirational recovery from cancer.[1] Far more memoirists and historians emerged from Team Europe. Seve, Monty, Torrance (two books), Faldo, Langer, James, Woosnam, Gallacher, and Feherty[2] shared the details of family and career and their unresolved conflicts regarding the Battle of the Coast. I read these volumes before getting down to primary research, and from them expected to find roving bands of lawless red, white, and blue (and camo) patriots disguised as golf galleries and the entire event skewed to ensure an American victory. It wasn't like that. Sour grapes produce a bitter whine, but some of the gripes seem legitimate, such as the American embrace of militarism in times of athletic peril, the highlight video at the formal dinner, and the U.S. flag embroidered on most of the logoed merchandise.

As for the supposedly over-the-top (Langer's phrase) crowd behavior, at least a portion of it must be attributed to that singularly annoying chant. "U-S-A! U-S-A!" should just go away.

1 In addition to an autobiography, Zinger gave the world *Cracking the Code,* which followed his successful 2008 Ryder Cup captaincy, and purports to give lessons in business and life.

2 Feherty is a category apart, since he turned pro as a writer following his retirement as a golf professional, and his Ryder Cup history book was made more factual and even-handed by his American collaborator, James Frank.

The Europeans *really* hated it: "By sacrificing their sporting dignity amid such rampant, wild-eyed nationalism at Kiawah, the Yanks were always going to be Ryder Cup losers—no matter the result," reported the *Daily Star*, a London tabloid. "The gentlemen from Europe taught them a lesson in how to remain calm, courteous, and honorable under outrageous pressure, in contrast to the whooping, the 'high-fives,' and self-congratulation of the strutting Yanks."

Rubbish, say American veterans of '85 and '89 in England. Remember Lanny getting booed on the first tee at the Belfry, and his mom turning white? "They weren't unruly at all at Kiawah, not compared to European crowds," says Van Sickle. "American Ryder Cup fans are amateurs, compared to the Euros." Adds Jacobsen: "You're a big boy. You got in here on your merits; block out the distractions. And I never saw a kicked ball. I doubt that happened."

The most credible accusation of fan interference—regarding Irwin's drive on the final hole of the final match—may not be completely resolved in this book. I've looked at the tape a hundred times and I can't see a kick. Nor can I see how the ball wound up in the fairway.

●

What did the '91 Cup mean? As John Garrity wrote in *Sports Illustrated*, the War by the Shore settled nothing, yet provided a stage for greatness and great failure. "It's hard to see how the merits of pro golf in either the U.S. or Europe can be adjudicated by one swipe of Langer's putter," Garrity wrote. But "what recent Ryder Cups have proved is individual mettle, so perhaps we should start according Ryder Cup heroes the same respect we grant the winners of major tournaments."

As for the captains, Gallacher wrote a book called *Captain at Kiawah*. Stockton has not been similarly heard from. (He has, however, authored golf instruction books.)

A War by the Shore reunion of sorts occurred when the Ocean Course hosted the PGA Senior in May 2007. Funny the way it turned out: Tim Simpson, who was in line to replace any injured U.S. player but became the merest footnote when he didn't get a call, had a better tournament than any of the '91 Ryder Cup alums. He shot -2 for the four rounds, good for fifth place, behind the -9 shot by the winner, Denis "One N" Watson of Zimbabwe. O'Meara finished T-12, Beck, T-19, James, T-33, and Floyd and Irwin, T-44. Gallacher was invited but didn't play; Stockton shot 81-74 and missed the cut.

Before the tournament began, and with an eye on posterity, Kiawah Island Golf Resort PR director Mike Vegis induced Irwin and Stockton to sit for taped interviews. What had we seen? What did it mean? Vegis asked the right questions. Some of Hale's reminiscences about his duel with Langer appear in the final chapter of this narrative.

The Stockton in an upholstered chair in the Sanctuary was about to become famous again, as a putting instructor. He'd taken some lumps since '91. Dave would have served a second term as Ryder Cup captain but was passed over in '93 in favor of Tom Watson; and he heard a million complaints about how charged the atmosphere had been in '91.

Stockton: *Calcavecchia?* "He's the reason we won I think, personally. Not a person was commenting on Payne Stewart and Raymond Floyd [who were losing their singles matches, while Mark led over Monty throughout their match] but the fact that if Calc can do it, I can do it. We won by half a point, and he's the reason."

Azinger? "A real leader. Lanny Wadkins, Azinger, Payne Stewart, and I—the four of us would constantly talk in the preceding year. There wasn't a week that went by that we didn't talk about who to put with who and what we thought about different situations."

Lanny? "Bulldog. He did great. I intended to put him out first [in the singles] because he likes to play fast, but he was tired. I figured he'd run the legs off anybody. He told me he'd like to go later in the rotation."

Pavin? "The heart of the team."

Floyd? "A crucial part of the team. I handpicked him to go with Freddie Couples. Anyone I put with Raymond would look good. . . . I put Freddie with the toughest competitor I could think of. It was gonna change Freddie's outlook to a certain extent."

Levi? "Wayne and Judy were an integral part of the team."

Stewart? "Phenomenal part of the team. Surprised he didn't win his singles match. Major loss that he was not a Ryder Cup captain. Not his greatest week, but a true ambassador."

Pate? "If the accident hadn't happened, I could have mailed it in. . . . I'm really resentful of the fact that he and [Corey] didn't get a chance to show their true colors."

Beck? "Chip's never seen a bad day, or anybody he doesn't like. Just a go-getter, positive attitude, the whole thing."

O'Meara? "At one point [Saturday afternoon] I wanted him to play and he declined to play. No mention was made or anything, but I was short-handed without Pate playing. I didn't ask him twice."

"The PGA made a mistake when they called it the War by the Shore. To me, I had business I wanted to attend to. The Ryder Cup hadn't been here in six years. I just wanted to have the feeling that we cared. Some of the captains immediately following me [Watson] said, 'We want to get it back to being civil like it was before.' But I think American pride is a great thing. Yes, it was probably louder than a lot of other previous Ryder Cups . . . but I think showing the enthusiasm was good for us. My team did care. America did care."

There's another way to look at that long-ago weekend in September. If the Ryder Cup is golf's ultimate pressure cooker—and everyone agrees it is; and if the Ocean is golf's toughest course—and that title is more or less official now; and if there has never been a tournament or exhibition more fraught with emotion and national pride, then the '91 Ryder Cup must be considered for what it was—absolutely unique.

Without doubt, the landscape and logistics of big-time golf

have changed profoundly. "With European players getting into majors more easily, and World Golf Championship events, and the big-money tournaments in the Middle East, guys from both sides of the ocean have mingled a lot more," says Van Sickle. "That Tour versus Tour rivalry is somewhat lost when Paul Casey and Luke Donald and half the European team play the U.S. Tour full-time.

"And let's face it: The balance of power has swung. The U.S. won the Ryder Cup in '91, '93, '99, and 2008 by the narrowest of margins. The American arrogance is gone."

So, perhaps, that War by the Shore was less a part of a continuum than a thing apart, a once-in-a-lifetime laboratory of athletic stage fright. Every shot succumbed to or overcame the stress that washed ashore at Kiawah Island. The numbing tension came through the TV and in the newspapers and even in memory.

Defending my country by hitting a good one iron on the seventeenth at the Ocean while 20,000 patriots watch—just the thought of it makes me shake.

POSTSCRIPT

Within months of being soaked in champagne and seawater at Kiawah Island, U.S. Ryder Cup Captain **Dave Stockton** won the first of the fourteen events he would accumulate on the Senior PGA Tour. His career as an instructor also blossomed. Major champions Phil Mickelson and Rory McIlroy were among the many pros who put some pop in their putting under Stockton's guidance. He wrote a book called *Unconscious Putting* (2011).

Bernard Gallacher led the European Ryder Cup team twice more after the razor-thin loss at Kiawah Island. His side lost again in '93 at the Belfry at BPGA headquarters in England but won at Oak Hill in New York in '95. After seven losses as a player and two as captain, Bernard finally had his Cup.

Seve Ballesteros played again in the Ryder Cups of '93 and '95, then took the helm for the first-ever Cup in Spain, in 1997, at the Valderrama Course—which he had had a hand in remodeling—at the Sotogrande resort in San Roque, Andalusia. He opposed a man with whom he'd had considerable competitive friction, U.S.

Captain Tom Kite. Relying in part on a golf cart that could travel as fast as a race car, Seve rallied his team to a win. The Seve Cup—pitting teams from Great Britain and Ireland against continental Europe—debuted in 2000. But sadness tinged the final chapters of Seve's life. His putting touch disappeared, his full swing lost its magic, and his back began to ache. He and wife Carmen divorced in 2004. Seve died in May 2011 of a malignant brain tumor. He was fifty-four.

Like Seve, **Mark James** played in two more Cups, then was selected to lead Team Europe in the '99 event at the Country Club in Brookline, Massachusetts, near Boston. In the only Ryder Cup to approach the emotion and controversy of the one at the Ocean Course, Team Europe lost a very large lead in the final day singles and the Match. There were hard feelings.

Steve Pate was among the singles winners who led the United States comeback in '99—appropriate for the PGA Tour's 1999 Comeback Player of the Year. Pate won a Nationwide event in 2010 and now plays the Champions (formerly Senior) Tour.

In a lovely gesture following the long-made putt by Justin Leonard that effectively won the Cup for the United States in '99, **Payne Stewart** conceded a winning putt on the eighteenth green to Colin Montgomerie. Everyone agreed that Stewart would be a U.S. captain one day—but he lost his life in a private jet crash just weeks later. He was forty-two.

The Matches were delayed for a year following the terrorist bombings of 9/11; when they resumed at the Belfry in 2002, extra meaning and poignancy were attached to the ceremonies involving flags and anthems.

Sam Torrance—he'd been on the side for the loss in '93 and the win in '95—put the exclamation point on a very satisfactory Ryder Cup career in 2002. "They have one Tiger, but I have twelve Lions," Captain Sam said. The Lions won.

Torrance's erstwhile drinking buddy **David Feherty** discovered sobriety. A grateful world discovered what true wit sounded like coming from a TV golf commentator when he joined CBS Sports in 1997. Feherty became a citizen of the United States in 2010.

Helped by the Calcavecchia collapse at Kiawah in '91, by Stewart's sportsmanship in '99, and by his own ability to rise to the occasion, **Colin Montgomerie** never lost in eight Ryder Cup singles matches, and his overall record of twenty wins, nine losses, and seven ties is among the best ever. He and Faldo became the symbols of European ascendancy in the modern history of the Cup. "Funny, isn't it," Monty said, declaiming on a practice green at Firestone on the eve of the 2008 edition. "If it hadn't been for some strange occurrences in Boston ['99], Europe would have won six in a row." Montgomerie capped a brilliant Ryder Cup career when he captained the winning side at Celtic Manor in 2010.

Remember **David Gilford**? The mild-mannered cattle breeder who endured (with Faldo) one of the worst losses in Cup history, then had to sit out the singles due to Pate's injury—poor David became Europe's hero in '95. He sat out the first day, then on Saturday he won in the morning with Langer and then in the afternoon with Seve. He beat Brad Faxon in the Sunday singles.

It would have been fitting for **Lanny Wadkins** to have gone out on top as a winning captain—but he did not, as his boys lost in '95 at Oak Hill. And it would have been equally appropriate for **Nick Faldo** to conclude his Ryder Cup career as a winning captain, but his squad also was defeated, at Valhalla in Kentucky in 2008. Two of the greatest modern Ryder Cup players were linked in another way when, in 2006, CBS Sports fired Lanny and hired Nick as its lead golf analyst.

Hale Irwin and **Bernhard Langer** also remained connected, at least for a week. The day after their singles match at Kiawah, both boarded a plane bound for Germany, where they played in the BMW Championship in Stuttgart. Langer won, a remarkable bounce-back from the bitter disappointment of that final putt . . .

. . . a putt that can no longer be attempted. The green on the eighteenth hole at the Ocean Course was relocated closer to the beach in 2002.

That change and others—new pot bunkers and a bulkheaded marsh crossing on the second hole; a bit of fill-in of the marsh on the left side of number four; a great deal more grass grown on the perimeters of all the holes—were designed and supervised by Ocean Course architect **Pete Dye**. "I'm just glad to be part of the team," Dye said twice in an unsatisfying on-air interview with Johnny Miller during the '91 Ryder Cup. He was and remains much more than that: Dye is by far the most influential golf-course designer of the past fifty years.

After **Paul Azinger** captained the winning Ryder Cup team at Valhalla in Kentucky in 2008, he revealed his winning strategy: put "pods" of players with similar personalities in pairs for practice and place them in peril in the Match.

Most golfers decline gently in middle age, losing a yard at a time or a putt per round—but **Chip Beck** misplaced his game suddenly and completely. He missed forty-six cuts in a row in '97 and '98. After two years without a paycheck, other athletes would fall on their swords; Beck sold his big house and bought a small one, took a sales job with National Life of Vermont, and eventually regained his form with help from instructor Jim Suttie. Beck won $636,000 on the Champions Tour in 2011.

With Ryder Cup records of three wins and two losses in '93 and four and one in '95, **Corey Pavin** showed his incredible competitive mettle. The '95 U.S. Open champion captained the losing side in 2010.

José María Olazábal, winner of the Masters in '94 and '99, played in four more Ryder Cups, overcoming severe arthritis in his right foot. Olly ended his career as a Ryder Cup player with a bang in the 2006 event at the K Club, County Kildare, Ireland, when he and countryman Sergio García went two and zero (Olly won his singles match, too, over Phil Mickelson). Olazábal is the 2012 captain for Team Europe at Medinah.

Fred Couples won the next Major played after the War by the Shore, the 1992 Masters, and he played in the three subsequent Ryder Cups. Fred and Deborah divorced in '93; she committed suicide in 2001.

Even after the trauma at Kiawah, **Mark Calcavecchia** retained his ability to go very, very low: In his two wins in the Phoenix Open ('92 and '01), he averaged sixty-five per round. In 2009, at the RBC Canadian Open, he birdied nine holes in a row to set a record. He and Sheryl divorced; Calcavecchia married the euphoniously named Brenda Nardecchia in Italy in 2005. But he never won another Major, and insiders such as Chuck Cook think the stress-filled hour on Sunday at the Ocean Course took a permanent toll. "I wouldn't put much water in that bucket," says Irwin. "The other players don't think he was damaged." After all, Calc won $1,867,991 on the Champions Tour in 2011. His personality remained upbeat and friendly. And within his compound in Tequesta in Palm Beach County, Florida, he has a two-lane bowling alley. Near it is a refrigerator. With beer.

ACKNOWLEDGMENTS

Special thanks to my agent, Bill Earley, of William Earley Literary, Merion, Pennsylvania, and to William Shinker and Travers Johnson of Gotham Books.

John Strawn and Patrick Madden read chunks of the manuscript and told me to keep going or to consider getting a plumber's license, as needed.

Mike Vegis, public relations director of the Kiawah Island Golf Resort, could not have been more helpful. Great guy, too.

John Sampson, my brother, provided material and spiritual support. "Moto" is one in a million, an indispensable man to a lot of us.

Pat Morrow, ex of the Cuyahoga Falls, Ohio, Parks and Recreation Department, and now a resident of Summerville, South Carolina, spent many hours in the library on my behalf and carved out time to conduct field research with John and me when we came to Kiawah last summer. Pat gave me my first job out of college, running his municipal golf course; and when

I moved on to an assistant pro job in South Carolina, he hired my younger brother to replace me.

I also humbly thank the gentlemen who sat still for interviews.

The rest by geography:

Augusta: Danny Fitzgerald, Chris Gunnels, Nicole L. McLeod, Jayme Usry, Col. Tim Wright

Charleston: Tommy Braswell of *The Post and Courier*—very helpful and a terrific guy

Dallas: Linda G. Gossett, Win Padgett

Kiawah Island: George Frye, Jim Kelechi, Nate Ross, Bob Ogwa

Ladies and gentlemen, thank you. Thank you very much.

BIBLIOGRAPHY

Azinger, Paul, and Ken Abraham. *Zinger.* Grand Rapids, Michigan: Zondervan Publishing House, 1995.

Azinger, Paul, and Ron Braund. *Cracking the Code.* Decatur, Georgia: Looking Glass Books, 2010.

Ballesteros, Severiano. *Seve: The Official Autobiography.* London: Yellow Jersey Press, 2007.

Barrett, Connell. "The unfunny life of David Feherty" *GOLF Magazine* (January 2007).

Bath, Richard. "Colin Montgomerie interview: 15 minutes to spare" *Scotland on Sunday* (March 22, 2009).

Diaz, Jaime. "Regular Guy" *Golf Digest* (August 2002).

Dye, Pete, and Mark Shaw. *Bury Me in a Pot Bunker.* New York: Addison-Wesley Publishing, 1995.

Faldo, Nick, Bruce Critchley, and David Cannon. *Faldo: In Search of Perfection.* London: Orion Publishing, 1994.

Feherty, David, and James Frank. *David Feherty's Totally Subjective History of the Ryder Cup.* New York: Rugged Land, 2004.

Gallacher, Bernard, and Renton Laidlaw. *Captain at Kiawah.* London: Chapmans Publishers, 1991.

Hamer, Malcolm. *The Ryder Cup: The Players.* London: Kingswood Press, 1992.

Jacklin, Tony. *Jacklin.* London: Hodder and Stoughton, 1970.

Langer, Bernhard, and Stuart Weir. *Bernhard Langer.* London: Hodder and Stoughton, 2002.

Lawrenson, Derek. "Ryder hero who chose to leave it all behind" *Daily Mail* (September 8, 2008).

Maltz, Maxwell. *Psycho-Cybernetics*. New York: Pocket Books, 1960.

Montgomerie, Colin. ElizabethMontgomerieFoundation.org.

Montgomerie, Colin, and Lewine Mair. *The Real Monty*. London: Orion Books Ltd., 2002.

Newman, Bruce. *Sports Illustrated*. 1992.

Reilly, Rick. "High noon at Troon" *Sports Illustrated* (July 31, 1989).

Roberson, Doug. "Friday conversation: Johnny Miller" *Atlanta Journal-Constitution* (September 22, 2011).

St. John, Lauren. *Seve: Ryder Cup Hero*. Nashville: Rutledge Hill Press, 1997.

Stewart, Tracey, and Ken Abraham. *Payne Stewart*. Nashville: Broadman and Holman Publishers, 2000.

Tait, Alistair. *Seve*. London: Virgin Books Ltd., 2005.

Torrance, Sam. *An Enduring Passion: My Ryder Cup Years*. Edinburgh: Mainstream Publishing, 2010.

Torrance, Sam. *Sam*. London: BBC Books, 2003.

Woosnam, Ian, and Edward Griffiths. *Woosie*. London: CollinsWillow, 2002.

INDEX